ALSO BY JIMMY CARTER

SHARING
GOOD TIMES

Jimmy Carter

Simon & Schuster

New York   London   Toronto   Sydney

SIMON & SCHUSTER
Rockefeller Center
1230 Avenue of the Americas
New York, NY 10020

SIMON & SCHUSTER and colophon are registered trademarks
of Simon & Schuster, Inc.

Book design by Ellen R. Sasahara

For information regarding special discounts for bulk purchases,
please contact Simon & Schuster Special Sales at
1-800-456-6798 or business@simonandschuster.com.

Manufactured in the United States of America

1   3   5   7   9   10   8   6   4   2

Library of Congress Cataloging-in-Publication Data
Carter, Jimmy.
Sharing good times / Jimmy Carter.
    p.   cm.
1. Carter, Jimmy, 1924–   2. Carter, Jimmy, 1924– —Family.
3. Carter, Jimmy, 1924– —Philosophy.   4. Miscellanea.
5. Leisure—Miscellanea.   6. Conduct of life—Miscellanea.
7. Presidents—United States—Biography.
E873.2.C379   2004
973.926'092—dc22   2004051351

ISBN 0-7432-7033-9

To Mary Prince,
whom we love and cherish

CONTENTS

INTRODUCTION

I N THE PAST, I have written about history, political
science, religion, the technique of negotiation, outdoor
experiences, a novel about the Revolutionary War, a book
of poetry, and a presidential memoir—all fairly serious subjects.
This book is about the more challenging, relaxing, and enjoyable experiences that I have known—both at work and at play.
I have described personal hobbies, excursions to exotic places,
political campaigns, volunteer work, fishing, skiing, climbing
mountains, baseball, family vacations, and simply relaxed days
and nights with little to do except exchange memories and
ideas with family and friends across the years and across generations.

Few of these adventures have been especially newsworthy,
and I still enjoy some of them in solitude, but the main lesson I
have struggled to learn is that the experiences are more deep
and lasting sources of pleasure when they are shared with others.

It has not been easy for me to accept this fact. Perhaps like
most other people, I have had to overcome a self-centered incli-

nation to live on my own terms, sometimes obsessed with intense ambition, bringing others into the private recesses of my life only reluctantly. I've come to realize that even my loved ones and I could enjoy the same event without really sharing the essence of it, and that it takes a lot of effort to sense and accommodate the desires of others in a generous way. This lifetime of learning has paid rich dividends, for me and for those with whom I have learned to really share.

I hope that these personal experiences will prove to be a practical and inspirational guide to anyone desiring to stretch mind and heart, to combine work and pleasure, and to reach out to others.

SHARING
GOOD TIMES

A BOYHOOD IN ARCHERY

A S A LITTLE BOY, I lived within a protective cocoon, sharing all my experiences with other people. Our home was in an isolated farm community named Archery, and all our neighbors were black families. My father, Earl, was a hardworking producer of pine timber, corn, cotton, peanuts, pork, beef, milk, wool, and other agricultural products who tried to market everything possible at a retail level, directly to consumers. His income varied widely, depending on the weather or market values at harvesttime, both equally unpredictable. My mother, Lillian, served as a registered nurse, and her duties were either in the nearby Wise Sanitarium, where she was in charge of the operating room, or on private duty to patients in the hospital or in their own homes. Always on call, she knew in advance what her compensation should be: four dollars for twelve-hour duty in the hospital or six dollars for twenty-hour duty in homes. Her payment from most of the local families was always uncertain, rarely in cash and mostly in chickens, eggs, a shoat or two, or sometimes some highly flammable turpentine chips, with which we could most easily start fires for heating the house or cooking.

Since my parents were often away from home and I had little in common with my younger sisters, I spent most of my waking hours with my black playmates and their families. It seemed that our friendships were strengthened as we cooperated—and competed—with one another. These earliest years were when I truly shared almost all aspects of my life with others.

As the wonders of the world were revealed to us, none were really complete until A.D., Johnny, Milton, Edmund, and I had absorbed them together. The struggle of a newborn mule colt to stand alone on wobbly legs, the opening eyes of a litter of puppies, the death throes of an enormous wharf rat that had eaten a bait of strychnine, a long string of catfish from the nearby creek, a ram mounting a compliant ewe, or a ride in a new goat cart had only partial meaning to us little children until we had shared the experience with each other. There had to be the proffering of individual opinions, a thorough discussion, and then some kind of consensus before we could add one more item to our store of knowledge. It was as though ten eyes and five brains were acting in concert. When the time came in our legally segregated society, I had to go to school exclusively with other white students, but I was always eager to return home to be with my closest and permanent friends.

I came to realize that my life, of necessity, would be compartmentalized, and I carved out some areas of interest or pleasure that would be almost exclusively my own. As an avid reader, I discovered a new and private world. My primary request to Santa Claus and as each birthday approached was for books, and

I lost myself in them. Increasingly during the following years, I found that few of the elements of my school life were of interest to my playmates on the farm, but we still retained our close friendship and continued to spend afternoon hours during the school year and all day during vacations together.

There was no distinction among us because of our different colored skin or social status as we competed in boxing, wrestling, running, fishing, exploring, playing baseball, and working in the fields as we became increasingly able. Then, when we were about fourteen years old, my black friends began deferring to me—perhaps they were instructed to do so by their parents as we approached maturity—and the intimate sharing of our childhood was finally changed into merely enjoying the same events.

I didn't realize it at the time, but to a surprising degree, learning when and how to share experiences fully with others, even loved ones, would be a lifetime challenge for me. This was a virtue, like many others, that would have to be sought and learned with difficulty.

MY FATHER WAS MY HERO, and I watched his every move with admiration and a desire to emulate what he did. I observed with great interest how he arranged his schedule of work and play and how he shared with others. Daddy worked from before sunrise until dark, with ever-increasing responsibilities to manage his farming and merchandising business. This single-minded work habit of his prevailed from Monday morning until Saturday afternoon, but then it seemed that his character changed completely. Few things, even my mother's sometimes obvious preference to stay at home and rest from her duties as a registered nurse, were permitted to interfere with partying on Saturday night.

Daddy loved to go to the American Legion Hall, Elks Club, or friends' homes, or to entertain at our house. There was a superb hospital in Plains, and quite often, my parents' companions were the doctors and nurses who were considered the most respected and heroic citizens of the town and who seemed to share my parents' desire to have a good time on the weekends. I always dreaded the nights when it was my parents' time to play host, because it was impossible for my sisters and me to get any sleep until long after midnight, when the last guests finally decided to go home.

The tinny Victrola music wasn't loud enough to disturb us, even through the thin walls, but the raucous conversations increased in volume as the hours passed. There was one doctor, Sam Wise, who had lost a leg as a young man and who was the jolliest in the crowd. Unmarried, he was quite a ladies' man, dated the prettiest young nurses, and loved to dance. Every time his peg leg hit the floor, the entire house would shake. It always seemed doubtful to me that the structure, bought from Sears, Roebuck and Company, would survive.

Later, in 1938, Daddy decided that our house was inadequate for entertaining, so he decided to dam up a small stream about two miles from home, create a pond, and build a cabin on a high bank overlooking the water. I was old enough and proud to help with this construction. After that, our house was blessed with quiet times, but every now and then I was wakened early on Sunday morning to take a team of mules over to the cabin to pull one of the automobiles out of the water. I never chose to ask any questions, and only rarely would Daddy identify the owner who had attempted to leave the party without being able to see clearly where he was going. I should add that my father was a deacon and a dependable Sunday school teacher and was always present and on duty when the church bell rang a few hours later.

We called the cabin the Pond House, and for my last years in high school it became a favorite site for entertaining friends during our frequent but closely chaperoned parties. These were my most vivid memories of how my parents interwove—or separated—their hardworking professional lives and the pleasure of sharing other hours with their friends.

Some of the most memorable and cherished events of my youth were the all-too-rare times when I was included in my father's activities. Daddy was an outstanding tennis player, having learned as he grew up in downtown Plains, and he built a tennis court on our farm within a week after we moved there when I was four years old. Although it was not considered proper to go fishing or fire a gun on Sunday afternoons, the men would assemble for highly competitive tennis. They played matches two-out-of-three games and, if undefeated three times, had to retire and wait in line for another chance. Daddy taught me how to play at an early age, and, though I was better than the other boys in high school, I never won a set from my father, who always played at his fullest capability. It didn't matter that I took only a point now and then; just being on the court with him was enough sharing for me.

There were times during the year when farm duties were not

so pressing. Fields were first plowed, or "broke," as soon after New Year's as possible, and planting was not usually begun until March. Sometime in June or July came "lay-by" time, when crops were too large to plow, and the harvesting of corn, peanuts, or cotton was still several weeks in the future. The last crops were usually out of the fields and sold or in the barn by November. During these slow times there were some regular duties to perform, including milking cows, slaughtering livestock, cutting wood, and repairing fences, buildings, and equipment, but the regimens were relatively flexible.

Daddy was also an expert fisherman and hunter and eager to pursue these skills, mostly with other men. But even before I was able to compete on the tennis court, Daddy would sometimes take me hunting. For quail, I would just tag along behind him and an adult companion so that I was never in danger of being shot, always watching the bird dogs and eager to be the first one to shout "point!" when one of the dogs froze to indicate that the birds were just ahead. When they flushed, it was my job to watch where any of them fell, to be sure that no dead quail were lost in the briars and grass.

For doves, I was actually helpful, so this was much more gratifying. Before dawn, Daddy and I would go into a field with many other hunters spaced apart for safety. We would make a small fire to prevent frozen fingers, and I would watch carefully, call out when doves were flying toward us, and run to retrieve the fallen birds and bring them to our "stand." I was the only little boy whose father treated him this way, and I would sometimes get to school a few minutes late, being careful to leave feathers still clinging to my sweater. Being permitted to share in his world further elevated my father in my worshipful eyes.

At least once each year, Daddy would join friends and go off to someplace further south in Georgia to fish for a few days. The Little Satilla River and the Okefenokee Swamp were favorite destinations. On several occasions after I was about ten years old, he took me with him. I fished from the same boat and waded out into the same stream during the day, then went to bed early while the grown men had a few drinks and played poker. Again, not only was I highly honored and grateful as the only boy along, but I could see how enriched was my father's life by the things he did for recreation with his friends and, I hoped, with his boy.

BASEBALL

THERE WAS A CLASS D baseball team that played in Americus, ten miles from our home. This was the lowest rung on the ladder of organized baseball, for smaller towns and new or fading players, and my folks attended whenever possible. My father's brother, Alton, was a league director, always had tickets, and never missed a home game. There was a rigid custom in those days for players to start out in the boondocks, work their way up step-by-step through each higher level of skill, and eventually a very few would reach the big leagues. By then, they would be well known to small-town baseball aficionados.

The highlight of my parents' year was during lay-by time, when the farm workload was minimal. Mother used her personal friendships with the doctors to be away from the operating room or private patients, and she and Daddy were free to indulge their passion for baseball. My parents, my uncle Alton, and his wife would drive "up north" to spend a week or ten days almost totally immersed in major league baseball. In order to "see the world," they would go to a different city each year, rotating among Kansas City, Washington, Philadelphia, Chicago, St. Louis, New York, Cleveland, Cincinnati, Boston, Pittsburgh, and Detroit. Since travel was much slower then, the teams played longer home stands, and the travels from Plains were always timed for doubleheaders and especially interesting contests. There were no games on Sundays or at night, so my folks had plenty of time to explore the cities and enjoy the tourist attractions.

Uncle Alton was several years older than Daddy, and he operated a large mercantile establishment and traded mules and horses, so the brothers had very little professional relationship. In addition, Uncle Alton never danced or tasted whiskey in his life and wouldn't even drink dopes (Coca-Colas), so neither did they share any social life. It was clear to all, though, that these annual baseball excursions bridged gaps in the family and, in a strange way, even bound all of us younger Carters together. We children knew that these were the *best* experiences of our parents' lives, and they chose to share them. It was a lesson I never forgot.

My family inherited the fascination with baseball. Mama and Daddy happened to be present in 1947 when Branch Rickey brought Jackie Robinson from the Negro Leagues' Kansas City Monarchs to play his first game for the Brooklyn Dodgers, and Mama became a lifelong supporter of the team. She lived at our isolated Pond House during her later years, and we installed one of the first satellite antennae so she could watch her team play. When she went with us to Atlanta to sit in the owner's box with Ted Turner, she embarrassed all of us Braves fans with her piercing voice urging the Dodgers to victory. At some time during the game, all of their players would come by to speak to her, and she seemed to have a special relationship with Manager Tommy Lasorda. He told me that he often received telephone calls from my mother when she thought he made a serious mistake or didn't treat his players properly.

When my brother, Billy, joined me as a part owner of Carter's Warehouse, I usually came to the office before sunrise. Billy would be there at least an hour earlier and would read several newspapers and memorize statistics and results of the previous day's baseball games. Like my mother, he was a walking encyclopedia of minutiae about the sport, and after losing several bets, I refrained from any arguments with him on the subject. Mama always said, without dispute, that Billy was the most intelligent of her children, but some of her judgment may have derived from their shared knowledge of America's game.

EXCEPT FOR KEEPING UP with major league standings and listening to a few games on the radio, my involvement with baseball was limited during my early years in the navy, but that changed in 1951, when I was transferred from the Pacific Fleet back to duty in New London, Connecticut. We were introduced to the world of television. Screens had grown from the size of postcards to the size of a sheet of typing paper by the time we saw our first set in the lobby of the bachelor officers' quarters, and the program was a New York Yankees ball game. I knew that Rosalynn understood the rudiments of the sport, having watched our submarine crew play softball, but was surprised to learn that she had also attended a number of minor league baseball contests with my parents and my sister Ruth. We quickly decided to buy a television set, and she and I soon became avid Yankee fans. She knew the team better than I because she saw all the games, day or night, while I was on duty, and she shared her knowledge while we watched them together when I was at home. Twice we took a bus to the city to see our team in person.

We shifted our allegiance to the Braves when they moved from Milwaukee to Atlanta, and Rosalynn and I were present in 1974 when Hank Aaron made baseball history by hitting his 715th home run to break Babe Ruth's record. As governor of Georgia, I presented him with a special automobile tag, HR-715, to commemorate the occasion. We rarely miss a game even now, mostly on television, and my general well-being is strangely affected by the latest performance of the Braves.

One of my most memorable baseball experiences, however, involved the Oakland Athletics. I was invited by the owner of the A's, Walter Haas (whose family also owned Levi's), to attend one of their final games in 1988, when they were on the way to the World Series. Walter said he had a surprise for me, and when I arrived at the ballpark, Joe DiMaggio and I were seated together. We talked enthusiastically for seven innings about the Yankee team that Rosalynn and I had followed so avidly when I was a young naval officer stationed in Connecticut and New York. Old and cherished memories came alive again. Joe answered all the long-standing questions I had about Mickey Mantle, Phil Rizzuto, Yogi Berra, Whitey Ford, Allie Reynolds, and himself, and then, somewhat timidly, he asked, "Mr. President, may I ask you for a big favor?" I replied, "Of course, what is it?" He said, "Would you autograph a baseball for me?" I practically shouted, "Man, you've got a deal!"

I have acquired a good collection of autographed balls, but the most notable was one that I threw out to begin the All-Star Game when Rosalynn and I visited Cuba in 2002. Afterward, both Fidel Castro and I signed it, and I gave it to The Carter Center to be auctioned at our annual ski weekend. After spirited bidding from around the nation, it finally sold for $165,000!

MY AMBITION, USNA

I HAVE BEEN AMBITIOUS all my life. Even when I was five years old, I had a specific goal to achieve, instigated by my parents: to be the first member of our family to finish high school and go to college. It was during the Great Depression, cash money was very scarce in our South Georgia farm area, and the only free colleges we knew about were the military and naval academies at West Point and Annapolis. When asked what I wanted to be when I grew up, I didn't respond "policeman," "railroad engineer," "FBI agent," "John Dillinger," or "cowboy." Although my father had been a first lieutenant in the army in World War I, I had a favorite uncle still serving as a radioman in the navy, so like a parrot I would reply, "I want to go to Annapolis." Throughout my childhood, my parents and I remained totally committed to this goal.

Despite the best efforts of my father to use his political influence, I could not obtain an appointment to Annapolis when I finished high school, so I went to a nearby junior college while I bided my time, with an ever-waning likelihood of success. Just in case our local U.S. congressman would follow the lead of others and award this honor through competitive examinations instead of for his own political advantage, I concentrated on science and mathematics. I never signed up for a subject unless it was recommended in my little dog-eared booklet that described the qualifications for admission to the Naval Academy.

Instead of commuting ten miles every day from home to college on the Trailways bus, I lived in the dormitory, volunteered for night courses, and eventually was chosen to be special assistant to Professor L. R. Towson, who taught astronomy, physics, and chemistry. He was also the commanding officer of the local army reserve unit and had to drill his unit once a week, so I was responsible for teaching his freshman class in chemistry, with laboratory work in qualitative analysis. There were no opportunities for extra learning that I didn't pursue.

My father's political efforts eventually bore fruit, and our congressman agreed to give me an appointment after a second year of college if my grades were maintained at a high level. With a year still remaining, I decided to transfer to the Georgia Institute of Technology, where preparation for Annapolis would be much more advanced than in the local college. At Georgia Tech, I also signed up for the Naval Reserve Officer Training Corps, my first step in what was to be an eleven-year career in the U.S. Navy. It appears foolish to me now, but it seems that in those years I was always too busy fulfilling my military ambitions to take time off for vacationing or the normal pleasures of college years except the brief leaves during the war when I could be back home in Plains spending time with my family and some girlfriends.

NAVY LIFE

B EFORE MOVING from Plains to the farm as a small boy, I happened to live next door to a one-year-old baby girl named Rosalynn Smith, and it was too small a community for me not to know who she was as we progressed through school. Although she was three years younger than I and not in my more exalted social circle of older students, Rosalynn later became the closest friend of my younger sister Ruth. I guess I saw her hanging around our house when I was at home, but it was not until my senior year at the Naval Academy that I remember ever speaking to her.

I was dating a beautiful girl in a nearby town who happened to be Miss Georgia Southwestern College, but she had a family reunion the night before my last day of summer vacation in 1945. A friend and I were cruising around in his rumble-seat roadster looking for a blind date, and we picked up Rosalynn and Ruth and took them to a movie. The next morning when I entered the kitchen, my mother asked, "What did you do last night, since Annelle was not available?"

I replied, "I went to a movie."

"Who with?"

"Rosalynn Smith."

"Oh, what did you think of her?"

"She's the one I'm going to marry."

After I took Annelle home on the last night of my vacation, Rosalynn went to the train station with my family, shortly after midnight, to see me off to Annapolis. Our romance grew, and my parents brought her to Annapolis the following February for some social events to commemorate the birthdays of Washington and Lincoln. I asked Rosalynn to marry me, and she turned me down. She finally yielded to my urgent appeals by the time I was graduated in June, and we were married a month later.

AFTER MY GRADUATION from the Naval Academy, I devoted full time to my duties on an old battleship, the USS *Wyoming*. This almost singular commitment was a combination of demands from the navy and my own ambition to excel. As one of the most junior officers, I was assigned a multitude of duties that seemed to be the dregs of responsibilities, involving little knowledge or experience in fire control, gunnery, navigation, or engineering. In addition to being the photographic and education officer, I had the dreary duty as assistant to the supply officer, specifically in charge of ensuring that there were adequate rolls of toilet paper, brooms, soap, mops, and other cleaning supplies onboard when we sailed, and of struggling to keep the ship as clean as possible after almost forty years in service. The old ship leaked too much oil to be permitted into the inner parts of the naval base at Norfolk, and we had to anchor as far out in the bay as possible. The long boat trips severely limited time for liberty, and it was inevitable that we ensigns had the fewest opportunities to be with our families on weekends. I was determined to reach higher goals in my chosen profession and used this extra time onboard ship to learn more about my navy duties.

With a total income of three hundred dollars a month and spending more than half of this on apartment rent and my food on the ship, we had little money left for recreation even if the time had been available. I performed my navy duties, and Rosalynn took care of all the family responsibilities, including birthing and nurturing our baby boys as they arrived.

It seems almost incredible to me now, but my wife and I shared very little in those days in Norfolk except an intense love affair, with our mutual desire satisfied only during the all too rare days and nights when I was at home. I also loved our baby boy, Jack, very much and enjoyed being with him but assumed few responsibilities for his personal care. During our first few minutes together on liberty days, I would give Rosalynn very brief reports, often including some personal complaints about what I was doing on the ship. She listened dutifully and would let me know about the baby's progress, struggles to stay within her strict household budget, and any special problems that she may have been confronting. I just assumed that she was satisfied with this compartmentalized relationship.

I had forgotten how gratifying it had been to balance work and pleasure and to share experiences completely and intimately with my childhood playmates. My almost single-minded commitment to my shipboard duties rarely included my wife, and we seldom left our apartment even for overnight or weekend excursions. Our travel was limited mostly to pushing a baby carriage around the city streets near our apartment or riding the streetcar to and from the nearest shopping centers.

During my brief times away from the ship, I never wanted us to be burdened with the mundane duties of buying groceries, diapers, or other such necessities, so Rosalynn performed these tasks while I was at sea. She would take the baby with her, walk to the streetcar line, and ride it to the store. She could buy only as much as she could carry in one arm, then get someone to help her board the streetcar with a child and shopping bags to go home. When she returned to the corner near our apartment, she had to leave her purchases propped against a light pole, rush home with the baby, then hurry back to the streetcar stop, hoping the bags of groceries would still be there.

I presumed that Rosalynn could manage "her" responsibilities while I took care of "mine." My almost total obsession was with my career except for these all too brief personal relationships within our family. Always seeking the greatest challenges, I worked my way up to a newer ship, then won a coveted assignment to submarine school and then to a ship operating out of Pearl Harbor, Hawaii, and into the Western Pacific.

After Rosalynn and our son, Jack, joined me in Hawaii, it seemed that even the strict navy commanders encouraged us subordinates to plan for leisure time. In those days, we considered Honolulu a paradise focused on the pleasure of the navy, and submariners retained the special status they had enjoyed during the World War. Except for a few long cruises back and forth to the Western Pacific and the mainland seaports from San Diego to Seattle, our submarine operated in and out of Pearl Harbor five days a week. We would leave port quite early each morning and terminate our exercises in time to return to port by midafternoon. This left time for a poker game at the officers' club or a game of golf before suppertime, but I always went straight home.

For the first time in our marriage, we had a reasonable balance between my naval career and some personal pleasure. Since we now owned a new Studebaker automobile, we were free to enjoy the beauties of the island of Oahu. Along with some of the other navy wives, Rosalynn studied hula dancing, and I learned to play the ukulele. This was during the time when the instrument had been made famous and popular by Arthur Godfrey and his *Radio Breakfast Hour,* but my talents were limited to providing a steady rhythm with the simplest of tunes. Rosalynn, however, was generally recognized as the best of the *haole* hula dancers and can still be induced under special circumstances to demonstrate her skillful and enticing movements.

Perhaps it's not too surprising that our second son was conceived and born on the island. The navy nurses learned that he would be called James Earl Carter III and put a beaded bracelet on his arm that said "Chip Carter," a name he would carry for life.

Despite the seductive ambience of the islands, I never let recreational activities or family responsibilities interfere with my ambitions for advancement. I was determined to be the first member of my Naval Academy class to qualify as a submariner. This required a precise knowledge of every detail of the vessel, including fire control equipment, the various guns, navigation, tanks, valves, hydraulic and water lines, diesel engines, batteries, and the complex electrical power plant. Most of this study and the preparation of drawings and text for my official "qualification" notebook had to be done when I was not on watch, so my time at home was still limited.

During the Korean War, my ship was moved from Hawaii back to San Diego, where both home life and sea duty were very unpleasant. The city was overcrowded, the landlady of our small rented apartment interfered constantly in Rosalynn's personal affairs when I was at sea, and my times at home were even more limited than they had been in Norfolk. After a few months on this assignment I was sent back to the Atlantic Fleet.

Except for the brief interludes in Hawaii, during all these years of our young married life Rosalynn and I rarely found an opportunity for vacations or the enjoyment of leisure time together. I asked Rosalynn recently if she could recall any opportunities during those early years of our marriage for enjoyable outings, and she found it difficult to do so. Her response was, "We drove up into Canada once, went to the horse races in Saratoga, and when we were transferred back and forth from the Atlantic to the Pacific, I remember enjoying the trips across the country."

AS FOR SHARING IDEAS and making joint plans for the future, I had much closer ties with shipmates on my submarines than with Rosalynn and our family. People who have been engaged in military service will understand the reasons for this intimate relationship. There was an intensity of mutual commitment that bound us together in a unique way. Either during peacetime or when our country was at war, each routine maneuver was fraught with potential danger, and we knew that the lives of the entire crew depended on the performance of every officer and enlisted man. At the same time, there was an ongoing competition as we each attempted to excel in order to enhance his own career.

My first submarine, the U99 *Pompfet*, was one of a fleet of older boats that had helped to defeat the Germans and Japanese in the Second World War. After I had completed submarine school at New London, Connecticut, Rosalynn and our little son, Jack, remained in Plains with our parents, and I reported to my ship in Hawaii two days after Christmas 1948. We departed the next day for a long cruise to the western reaches of the Pacific Ocean. Having been burdened with multiple duties and constant written reports in my previous assignments on old battleships, and with the more pleasant but also demanding responsibilities of a husband and father, I felt a sense of almost total liberation when we cleared the last channel buoy and headed for the open sea. For months I would be encapsulated in this overcrowded, cigar-shaped tube of steel with seventy-one other men, my senior officers able to communicate only spasmodically with the outside world through the navy's long-range radio system. We would be almost constantly at sea, sometimes operating with other ships and spending a few rare days alongside a dock on an isolated island or in a coastal city of China, while taking on fuel and other supplies.

In those days, before snorkels permitted our diesel engines to run while we were submerged and when nuclear power was not even a dream, a submarine spent most of its time on the surface, propelled and charging batteries with its diesel engines. At top speed, our battery would last only thirty minutes, so we had to husband its power by proceeding very slowly during daylight hours, surfacing under the cover of night to recharge the batteries and to move long distances at higher speed. To compensate for this extremely restricted and often dangerous life, the navy had long sought to give submariners every possible reward, including 50 percent extra pay, the best food available, more commodious living quarters for our families ashore, and the exalted status of an elite fighting force.

When not on duty, we had a supply of the latest sixteen-millimeter movies, a good library of small-size books, and ongoing games of cribbage, bridge, chess, checkers, and poker. Perhaps because one of my early duties was as supply officer, the memorable events for me involved getting food for the crew. When there were heavy flights of flying fish as we cruised on the surface at night, we would erect our heavy canvas movie screen, illuminate it with a spotlight as an attraction, and pick up enough fish to feed the entire crew. Once we encountered a lobster boat far from its home port, and with its crew tired of eating seafood, I swapped a case of canned peaches for seventy-two of their catch.

In U.S. Navy ports at Midway Island and Guam, the officers would usually go to our fairly exclusive clubs and the enlisted men to their clubs or to local taverns. In Hong Kong, Shanghai, or Tsingtao, there were exotic souvenirs to buy for wives and sweethearts, and the companionship of prostitutes was always available for those who wished it. Sometimes we would borrow jeeps or motor scooters for sightseeing excursions to the surrounding communities. A common denominator was excessive drinking, and some of the highly inebriated officers and enlisted men had to be brought back aboard for their own protection.

As the Korean War progressed, we were ordered back to San Diego, and after a few months there I was assigned to complete construction of the first ship the navy was to build after World War II. This was a small "killer" boat, designed to operate with extreme silence and equipped with a massive sonar array that could hear and analyze the sounds of ships at a great distance. Our exclusive role was to destroy Soviet submarines with our torpedoes long before they were aware of our presence.

The officers and crew of the *K-1* were even more intimately intertwined than those on the *Pomfret*. With four officers and fewer than fifty men onboard, there was little room for physical separation, and we were also bound together while onshore. This time, operating out of New London, in the Caribbean, and along the Atlantic Coast, our crew members were much more restrained by the proximity of our families and therefore led a more staid social life. One good addition was an emphasis on competitive sports, and we fielded one of the outstanding softball teams in the submarine fleet. Our success depended primarily on the prowess of Petty Officer Russell, who had a fast pitch that was accurate and almost unhittable. To win, we other players just had to score a run or two. The only opposing team members to reach first base were the rare ones who swung their bats blindly and accidentally intercepted the ball. With an easygoing manner and a big smile, Russell was the most popular man on the boat.

Despite differences in rank, the members of our crew joined in many recreational activities as well as shipboard life on a submarine, and it did not seem strange to me that my closest friends happened to be enlisted men. One was a hospitalman's mate who shared my love for fishing. He and I spent many hours, on weekends or all during cold winter nights, casting or trolling for striped bass. There was also a quartermaster whose navigational skills and knowledge of the heavens exceeded mine with whom I had a friendly competition on the identification of stars and the accuracy of fixing our geographical positions from sextant observations. Our captain, Frank Andrews, took every opportunity for the entire crew to enjoy each other's company, and there were frequent picnics and other outings for all the wives and children while we were in port. Despite all this, however, we all realized that home life and navy duties would always be separate and somewhat in conflict.

From the *K-1,* I was awarded the most highly coveted assignment in the submarine fleet: to work under Captain Hyman Rickover in the development of the first two ships that would be propelled by nuclear power. We were transferred to Schenectady, New York, where General Electric Company was building the full-size prototype of a plant that would use liquid sodium to be pumped into the radioactive core and bring out heat to operate the steam-driven submarine propulsion system.

All of these complex interrelationships with others in the navy formed a major and almost totally sequestered facet of my life. I kept Rosalynn informed about my plans for the next steps in my career and on my daily activities but never considered it necessary to seek her advice or approval. It seemed that I was always busy, and except for my solitary running and other routine exercise, and a rare evening out with our family in a restaurant, there was little time for recreation.

Despite this, we both agree that our seven years as a young navy couple evoke only pleasant memories, which are unmarred by the abrupt and dramatic change in the course of our lives. We had no premonition of the political and other adventures that awaited us.

BACK TO PLAINS

I WENT HOME to spend a few days at his bedside when my father was terminally ill with pancreatic cancer, and even to my own amazement, I decided to retire from the submarine force and return to Plains—without any consultation with Rosalynn! My reasons for deciding to end my navy career are still not completely clear to me. There is no doubt that a major factor was the comments of a stream of well-wishers who came by my parents' home to pay their last respects to my father. I was amazed at the profound impact of his life on theirs, as he had fulfilled his role in a multiplicity of community affairs. His private acts of kindness and generosity, many of them unknown even to my mother, were impressive. He was a state legislator and a leader in education, health, agriculture, youth activities, business, and community development. Still fun-loving and active in sports, he and my mother had a wide circle of friends with whom they enjoyed times for recreation.

I relished the quiet ambience of the town, with its apparent stability and the intimacy of its few citizens, who came together naturally in times of sorrow, challenge, or celebration. It was also a special pleasure to be reunited with the friends of my childhood and to share memories of those bygone days in Archery.

Ultimately, it was a choice between an uncertain but potentially expanded life back home and a predictable and successful career in the U.S. Navy, narrowly focused on an ultimate goal of high rank and then a pleasant retirement. My unilateral decision to return home (I didn't accept any argument) became a divisive factor in our marriage. Rosalynn was furious, having learned to relish her independence as a navy wife. She wept and cajoled, but I exerted my dominance as a husband, and we closed the door on my naval career and headed back home. Rosalynn hardly spoke to me during the thousand-mile drive from Schenectady.

We had three little boys, no money saved except a few war bonds, and I would be operating a small business in partnership with my mother and, much later, with my brother, Billy, who had been only three years old when I left home for college. In October 1953 we moved into a small apartment in a government housing project in Plains, and I began to settle my father's estate and relearn what I had forgotten about how to produce crops on my one-fifth portion of the family farm. Our total income was less than three hundred dollars during our first full year at home, both because of a drought and because our moderate stance on the race issue alienated many of my father's former customers at our warehouse. I had no need for regular employees, being able to load whatever fertilizer, seed, and pesticides I could sell. I would hire a street lounger for an hour or two to help me when I had to unload a forty-ton shipment of fertilizer from a boxcar into our storage house.

Carter's Warehouse did better during 1955, with a net profit of $3,300, and I began to need help with recording sales, tracking inventories, monitoring accounts receivable, and billing customers. Rosalynn volunteered to help me during the afternoons, and we began to form a real partnership for the first time in our marriage on anything other than our personal family responsibilities.

This meant that both of us were involved closely in the daily lives of our children, at home and at school. As soon as our three boys were old enough to work, we assigned them responsible tasks in the fields and at the warehouse. In order to be certified as producing pure and superior seed, our peanut fields had to be free of aberrant varieties and weeds. It was within the capability of even a six-year-old to walk back and forth along the rows and pull up any plants that were not supposed to be there, and just a glance from my pickup truck would reveal any omission in performing their duties.

Once harvested and sealed in distinctive bags, each lot of seed peanuts had to be identified, and our boys could match lot numbers well enough to attach the proper labels. When older, they could monitor the drying and curing of peanuts, a round-the-clock, seven-day-a-week task during harvest season, and could also drive trucks to spread fertilizer in customers' fields. Of necessity, we had a close-knit family partnership—obviously, with me as boss.

Our work was constant and difficult, with the unending strain of growing crops and selling farm supplies in a competitive market, attempting to purchase harvested crops both to be a source of income and to ensure that farmers settled their accounts, repairing our complex machinery, and operating an extensive farming operation.

All of this was reminiscent of my father's life, and I began to emulate his decision to combine pleasure with work, at least on weekends and during slack seasonal times. In addition to some annual excursions, Rosalynn and I fished the creeks on Saturday afternoons, turned the little boys over to a babysitter, and then enjoyed being with a few close friends of ours until the early hours Sunday morning. Like Daddy, I was a Sunday school teacher and a deacon in our church, and always there when the bell rang.

Instead of following my parents' habit of annual vacation visits to big cities where they could combine daytime baseball games with other entertainment, we planned pleasure trips with another farm couple who shared our love of jazz and other music. We pooled our available funds at the beginning of each trip, and I usually acted as treasurer, paid all the bills, and announced when we were approaching insolvency and would have to return home.

One of our most memorable visits was to New Orleans, where I remember that our total bankroll was six hundred dollars. We found inexpensive hotel accommodations and spent most of our nights in the Bourbon Street and Royal Street nightclubs that had the best jazz performers. In one of them, we formed a special friendship with Billy Eckstine, and we later invited him to visit us in the White House. We had coffee and sweet rolls in the French Market early every morning before going to bed to sleep until early afternoon. During two of our days, we obtained permission from the New Orleans Symphony manager to sit in the theater during their practice sessions, and on the other days we went to horse races and toured the cemeteries, waterfront, and other tourist attractions. We decided that we would splurge one night and have supper at Antoine's Restaurant, where we enjoyed pompano cooked in a paper bag (seven dollars) with potato slices that swelled up like small balloons. We then went to dance in the Blue Room above the Fairmont Hotel, and subsequently we would call long-distance from Plains to make special requests for our favorite songs.

In 1958 we drove to Miami, where Louis Armstrong was performing in the Fontainebleau Hotel, and we remember our astonishment when the stage rose from below the dance floor with him and his orchestra playing their initial song. While on the beach the next day, we made a spontaneous decision to go to Cuba and were soon on the way. We stayed in Havana for two days, casually noticing that the palace of the dictator, Fulgencio Batista, was surrounded by soldiers and stacked sandbags and that many people were talking about a revolutionary lawyer named Fidel Castro, who was hiding in the hills. Since we had hotel rooms for only the first night, we spent the next one carousing in Havana and then flew without sleep to Miami the following day and drove back home.

The next year we went to Baltimore, primarily to hear performances by Sarah Vaughan. One evening happened to be especially memorable because the nightclub's sound system failed, and the audience sat in almost absolute silence for two hours, except for sustained applause each time she finished a song.

Rosalynn and I joined a group of square dancers in the mid-1950s and learned additional steps each week. Once or twice a year, we went to a statewide convention of square dancers, where we formed close friendships that were quite valuable when I surprised even myself by running for public office.

These activities, at work and play, required a lot of mutual agreements, and really for the first time, I was beginning to consult with Rosalynn and to accommodate her ideas and preferences before final decisions were made. I learned that real sharing was much more than laboring together at the warehouse or even dancing all night with each other and with friends. It included planning in advance and later savoring our experiences. What was especially challenging but enjoyable was treating my wife—and even sometimes our boys—as equal partners, with mutual respect for their opinions and with special delight in their pleasure. This did not come easy for me.

TRAVELING WITH OUR BOYS

HAVING THREE BOYS, I couldn't emulate the intimate relationship with my father that I had cherished when I was his only son and he took me along on his fishing and hunting excursions with other men. Instead, Rosalynn and I had to find opportunities for recreation with three growing boys. We spent weekends at Panama City Beach on occasion, and each year in the early summer we would drive down to Tavares, Florida, with two other farm families for a week of competitive fishing. We rented small boats and three rustic cabins alongside Lake Harris and would spend almost the entire day on the lake, leaving one of the adults ashore with the smallest children. Using our own gasoline motors, we would race early each morning to a favorite fishing spot, perhaps under a bridge, near one of the islands, or in an area of lily pads, and use long and slimy pond worms to entice bluegill bream and largemouth bass to our hooks.

Back to the cabins at noon, and late in the afternoon, we paid off bets, weighed our catch, bedded in ice what we wouldn't be cooking, and joined in preparing our common meals. In the evenings, after the children were asleep, we had long discussions about fishing, farming, politics, and baseball, and then put on our favorite phonograph records and danced until the early morning hours.

We were quite concerned as we were coming in to dock one day and saw a large crowd gathered, waving their arms and shouting to us. We immediately assumed that one of the little children had had a serious accident but soon learned that five-year-old Chip had been fishing with a tiny cane pole and about six feet of string and, after a long struggle, had dragged a huge bass up on the beach. We took photographs of him with his fish and me alongside with one of my tiniest ones. Almost fifty years later, this still stands out as one of the most exciting moments in our family's life.

As an outdoorsman since childhood and as Boy Scoutmaster when my sons were schoolboys, I took them on occasional overnight camping trips, and our entire family had two major sojourns of this kind. Designed to knit us together as closely as possible, our first was a weeklong trip around Georgia, camping out each night in a different state park, either in the mountains or along the seashore.

The other was more extensive, lasting almost two weeks and extending through the Carolinas, Virginia, Delaware, Maryland, and the District of Columbia. We resolved before leaving home that we would depend mostly on our fishing rods and swimsuits for recreation, sleep in our tent, cook our own meals on a Coleman stove, and divide up the chores so that each of us would have specific responsibilities.

With the exception of three destinations, we did not have any fixed itinerary but would decide in a family council each night what we would do the next day. Rosalynn and I wanted to visit the U.S. Naval Academy, do some sightseeing in Washington, and find the cabin in North Carolina where we had spent our honeymoon. Although we thoroughly enjoyed the camping experiences, our most lasting memory of the trip is that it rained almost constantly, and neither our tent nor any of our other possessions ever had a chance to dry. We'll always remember the stench of the mildewing tent in the back of our station wagon and the difficulty of starting a campfire in the evenings.

Annapolis was a wonderful stop for me, because I was able to introduce my boys to the Naval Academy and act as a knowledgeable guide. After I identified myself at the office as an alumnus, we received a pass to visit throughout the campus and to use one of the knockabouts for an afternoon of sailing. This was where I had asked Rosalynn to marry me and, after she finally accepted, where I had given her a miniature of our class ring during the week of my graduation.

By the time we reached Washington, we were badly in need of hot showers and a couple nights of sleep in beds. We all remember Rosalynn and the boys finally convincing me to abandon our tent and shift to a hotel. We drove our muddy vehicle up to a very large and new Marriott Inn across the Potomac River in Virginia, and I went in to ask about the nightly rates. When the desk clerk told me that it would cost twenty-six dollars for five people, I responded that we would have to stay in our tent and started to leave. He asked what we could afford, and we finally agreed on eighteen dollars. The luxurious accommodations were worth the high cost, and our tent had dried out by the time we headed for the Appalachian Mountains and our old honeymoon site.

Rosalynn and I had spent our first nights together in a lonely cabin on a mountainside owned by the family of another midshipman. It was several hundred yards down a steep trail to a small family grocery on the highway, but we bought most of our groceries that week from a traveling store mounted on an old pickup truck that came by the cabin each day. When not just enjoying the intimacy of our new relationship, we would take long hikes along the mountain trails or ride a few miles to Chimney Rock, a nearby tourist site. We were eager to share some of these memories with our boys.

When we finally found the place, using some old photographs, we found that it had been totally transformed into a rapidly growing community of weekend vacation cabins and permanent residences for retired people. The country store was gone, replaced by a small shopping mall. After a brief and somewhat disappointing visit, we went to nearby Lake Lure for a shower in the public bathhouses before heading back to Plains.

IN 1965, when our oldest son, Jack, finished high school, we planned a wandering trip through Mexico, and before leaving home, I tried to teach the family a few Spanish phrases from my Naval Academy textbooks. We left Plains in our Buick sedan with no plans made except having studied a map and some travel brochures. Part of the adventure would be deciding each morning where we wanted to travel during that day.

We still have a detailed log of the trip, mostly written by Jack and with Rosalynn, Chip, and me substituting while Jack was driving. It is filled with humorous observations, including a lot about my penny-pinching restraints on their expenditures, and it is interesting now to recall how inexpensive travel was in those days and how obsessed we were with prices. While we were still in the United States, for instance, our total costs for night lodging were usually ten dollars, and less than four dollars for our five meals.

Our boys were surprised that folks had a French accent in southern Louisiana, that there were trees in Texas, that many rivers were completely dry, and how nonproductive the land seemed to be, with one cow for forty acres of land. Accustomed to lush pastures at home, Jack commented south of San Antonio, "Cows run around in groups of one."

We were determined to try our Spanish when we entered Mexico but at first had little success. One of our first stops was at a small rural church where we saw a priest with a group of little children. We approached him, and using my best Spanish to impress my family, I said, *"Su iglesia es muy bonita."* The boys howled with laughter when the priest looked puzzled and responded, *"Me siento, pero no hablo inglés."* Jack's log has a detailed account of the first time a clerk understood what he wanted to buy and gave him the price. Our Spanish improved with every stop, at least using the few necessary words, and we were soon having conversations with little trouble. I required each of the boys to order his meal in Spanish. Our notes emphasize how friendly and helpful all the people we encountered were and how they enjoyed hearing our Spanish—except in the banks, where tellers seemed to be sullen and resentful when our only transaction was to exchange our traveler's checks for cash.

There was a tiny home every five miles or so along the country roads, very few cars, and a lot of burros. South of Saltillo, we passed a crude sign that said, "Los Llanos," with an arrow pointing to a cluster of distant shacks. I announced that it meant "Plains," and the boys insisted that we stop and back up for a photograph. Our car was surrounded by a half dozen very aggressive little children, shouting and holding out their hands. I told Rosalynn to find a few coins to answer their demands, but we finally understood that they were not asking for "dinero." Their words were *lápiz* and *papel*. We gave them some pencils and paper and drove away marveling at their priorities.

In San Luis Potosí we decided to mail our log home instead of writing letters, and Jack began writing on both sides of the tablet pages to save postage in the future. Near Querétaro, the log's comments are about the ancient stone walls, perhaps several thousand years old, and "the black earth that has probably been here even longer." In Mexico City, our log dwells on the game of jai alai, the Museum of Anthropology, and "limonada preparada." I let the boys drink all they wanted, and our family spent 29 pesos at one sitting for the limeade with sherbet. After visits to the ruins and a drive to Acapulco, we returned through Taxco, where we found the highest hotel prices. One wanted 225 pesos for our family, but we finally found a nice one, the Menendez, for just 85. It was on such a steep hill that our room was on the first floor in front and six stories above the backyard. Everyone agreed that Taxco was our favorite city visited in Mexico.

We also went to San Juan del Río and then Ciudad Victoria, where we attended a Yugoslav folk opera and saw that the London Philharmonic would be coming soon. These were international cultural events sponsored by the government and priced so everyone could enjoy them, with tickets costing from one to five pesos. Then we drove through Monterrey, McAllen, and back home.

Quoting from our boys' journal: "It has been gratifying how our family has seemed to enjoy everything and each other. We've had good and bad accommodations, been tired and rested, clean and dirty, free-spending and penny-pinching, and it has all been pleasant and interesting. Being able to speak Spanish has helped a lot. Some of the poorest Indians have never known anything except a few acres of cactus and a small herd of goats, but we don't feel at all sorry for them. A prevalent motto on walls and buildings is 'Libertad y Agua.' They are deeply religious and their children are learning to read and write. Hundreds gather around a small mariachi band for hours, and they are familiar with the art of Orozco, Rivera, and O'Gorman. What has impressed us most is their love for the land and pride in their ancient culture. We've noticed that in the lush climatic regions there are very few cathedrals."

LEARNING ABOUT POLITICS

TRUE SHARING OF my personal life with others has not come naturally to me, and on a larger scale, it has been a very difficult thing for our entire nation. For a hundred years after the abolition of slavery, white and black citizens chose to avoid sharing even the basic elements of life—a decision upheld by the U.S. Congress and confirmed legally by the Supreme Court. It is embarrassing now to recall how few challenges were ever mounted during those generations of "separate but equal" coexistence, from either black activists or white idealists. I have to admit that I accepted racial segregation, along with its debilitating discrimination, with relative equanimity. During those years our black neighbors were required to attend school and ride on public vehicles separately, yet they could not exercise the duties of citizenship by voting or serving on a jury.

During my first thirty-eight years, I never contemplated running for office but had only two successive professional goals: to be a career naval officer and, after my father's death in 1953, to be a successful farmer and businessman. In an attempt to con-

tinue his legacy in public service, I assumed a number of community responsibilities, including deacon and teacher in our
church, Boy Scout leader, district governor of Lions Clubs,
member of the regional hospital authority, chairman of the Georgia Planning Commission, and chairman of the Sumter County
Board of Education.

This was during the time of racial turmoil in the South, and
our Plains community was not immune to the discord that
threatened to permeate our region. I had first experienced this
evolving tension when I came home on leave from my submarine
in 1950 and described the beneficial changes that had resulted
from President Harry Truman's order to end racial segregation
throughout the armed services. It is important to remember that
this courageous and extremely controversial executive order was
issued more than five years before Rosa Parks decided to sit in the
front of the bus in Montgomery and launched Martin Luther
King's notable career as a civil rights leader.

We had made the transition to racial integration on the
USS *K-1* without any trouble among our crew members but
had an unfortunate confrontation with British officials when we
visited Bermuda. The governor-general sent an invitation to our
submarine crew to attend a ball at his official residence, and his
aide who delivered the message commented to me that the
young ladies in the community were looking forward to meeting some of our American officers and crewmen. Our captain
accepted the invitation, and excitement built as the day for the
party approached.

I happened to be the officer of the deck when the governor's
aide returned to our ship with a follow-up message, and I es-

corted him to the wardroom to speak to our captain. With no embarrassment, he stated that we must understand, of course, that the invitation did not include any nonwhite members of the crew. One of our most popular crew members was an African American, the petty officer named Russell who happened to be the best softball pitcher in the Atlantic Fleet. Within an hour, the chief of the boat came to tell the captain that the crew had decided unanimously to reject the invitation and wanted a response delivered to the British officials. There was not much left of the crew's message after the expletives had been deleted, so a brief and polite declination was sent from the ship.

When I related this incident to my parents, my father expressed agreement with the governor-general and left the kitchen. Mama said that she agreed with President Truman, but she reminded me that racial integration was not a proper subject to be discussed with Daddy or any other white people in the Plains community. In fact, this was a moot question in those days when "separate but equal" was the undisputed constitutional premise on which the social, educational, and judicial life of our entire nation was based.

Ten years later, after we had returned to Plains, our family's relatively modest acceptance of racial integration had aroused strong criticism among some of our neighbors. Abusive signs were tacked to our door, and a large group of my father's old friends came to encourage me to join the White Citizens' Council, a nonviolent offshoot of the Ku Klux Klan. After I refused, there were months when most of our customers quit coming in to buy fertilizer, seed, or other agricultural supplies from Carter's Warehouse. We were facing a business failure, and I was contemplating the possibility of returning to a civilian job I had been offered in the nuclear power industry.

A turning point in Georgia may have been indicated in our church one Sunday when a vote was called on whether to allow black people to enter our sanctuary for worship. The church sanctuary was uncharacteristically filled with our members, and after I made a brief speech our family and one other person voted to welcome any worshipers, while there were fifty votes in opposition. The significant thing was that more than a hundred people didn't vote, and many of them called our home that afternoon to say they agreed with us.

AFTER ALMOST NINE YEARS at home, we were finally enjoying a thriving business, with productive farmland and a comprehensive farm supply operation built around the processing and sale of high-quality seed peanuts. We were enjoying some vacations and weekend parties, and our family worked together at the warehouse. Still, I was not inclined to share other important and basic decisions with the wife I loved. She and I have often discussed the most vivid example of this strange relationship, including the early morning of my birthday in 1962. When I began to dress, I laid aside the usual work clothes and began to put on my Sunday suit.

It was a Monday, and Rosalynn asked, "Is there a funeral or something today?"

I replied, "No. I'm going to the county courthouse and qualify to run for the state senate."

It is almost incomprehensible to both of us now, but I had

never discussed this life-changing decision with her. After I was finally elected, following one of the most bizarre political campaigns in Georgia history (described in my book *Turning Point*), I spent several months in Atlanta each year, and Rosalynn operated the warehouse, now knowing as much about our business as I. She and I also began to have regular discussions of the political decisions in which I was involved.

My hasty and almost solitary campaign for the state senate had come after the "one man, one vote" Supreme Court ruling in 1962, but our entire family did not begin participating in politics until the presidential campaign two years later. As a proponent of civil rights, Lyndon Johnson had become quite unpopular in the Deep South and deliberately wrote off our region. He never campaigned in Georgia, Alabama, Mississippi, or Louisiana and preferred to be known as a Midwesterner, not a Southerner. Nevertheless, my mother volunteered to be his campaign manager for Sumter County. She persevered despite having scurrilous messages written on her automobile and knots tied in its antenna. She was later delighted to be a delegate to the national convention in Atlantic City.

Following Mama's lead and without any encouragement from us, our sons also participated in their own ways. Chip has always been most interested in politics, and he put a Johnson-Humphrey button on his shirt and an I AM A DEMOCRAT sticker on his notebook. He came home from school several times with his shirt torn and evidence of combat, but he remained staunch in his loyalty. Finally, though, he returned in tears after one of his classmates pulled his chair from under him at glee club practice. He exclaimed to us, "I'm not going to be a Democrat anymore!" But the next morning he wore an LBJ button and had a new sticker on his notebook. (Johnson lost only the four southern states and Arizona, the home state of his opponent, Barry Goldwater.)

AFTER A THOROUGH DISCUSSION with Rosalynn, I made a last-minute decision to run for governor two years later. Most of the extremely brief campaign was conducted during lay-by time in the early summer, and Rosalynn and one of our sons would ride from one town to another, handing out pamphlets, visiting local radio stations and newspaper offices, and intruding on regular meetings of Lions, Rotary, Kiwanis, Civitan, and other civic organizations. She learned about the intensity of political commitments the hard way, when a supporter of one of my opponents spat directly in her face. With her personal experiences on the campaign trail, Rosalynn became a permanent and incisive participant in the strategy sessions of our political advisers.

SHARING MY FAITH

HERE WERE A NUMBER of candidates in the 1966 Democratic primary, but the most colorful was Lester Maddox, an avowed segregationist who gained fame by threatening to use the handle of a pickax on any black person who dared to enter his restaurant for service. A distinguished former governor, Ellis Arnall, also ran, as did several other men who had long been on the Georgia political scene. I was a newcomer, filled with a sense that it was my destiny to "save the state of Georgia and the public school system." I lost the race by a narrow margin, and also lost faith in my own ability, the political system, and God's will for my life.

Hearing about my disillusionment, my sister Ruth Carter Stapleton came from her home in North Carolina to talk to me. A famous evangelist, author, and amateur psychologist, she recommended that I forget about politics and the competitive business world for a while and dedicate myself to some religious or altruistic goals. At first I ridiculed her optimism, but I finally decided to take her advice. More than at any other time in my life,

I immersed myself among other Christians and volunteered to go on a series of what we called "Pioneer Missions." This was another phase of my learning to share with others.

My first experience, in Lock Haven, Pennsylvania, is typical of those I had on all these trips to explain my faith to many kinds of people, most of whom were known to be nonbelievers. My partner was Milo Pennington, a Texas farmer who had not finished high school but was experienced in this voluntary mission work. He and I agreed that he would give the basic explanation of our Christian faith, and I would help with scripture readings and assist in answering any questions that might arise. A group of Baptists at Pennsylvania State University had called everyone listed in the Lock Haven phone book and gave us the names and addresses of a hundred families who had reported that they never attended religious services of any kind. Our assignment was to visit all of them, describe the "plan of salvation," and if possible, establish a permanent group of committed Christians who would continue to worship together.

Milo and I found an inexpensive double room in the local YMCA and began our visitations. As we approached each home we would pause for a prayer, knock, introduce ourselves, explain our mission, and seek to have a conversation. Our list varied from a wealthy automobile dealer to a prostitute who lived above some stores in a run-down part of town. Sometimes we were sent away abruptly, but most of the people let us deliver our message. It was an incredible experience for me to forget completely about my own timidity or pride, not be concerned about the eloquence of our presentation, and place the responsibility for results completely in the hands of God.

Our message was often rejected, but forty-eight people had accepted Jesus Christ as Savior when we finally completed our assignment. Before leaving Lock Haven, we helped them find a building to use as their new church.

A later assignment was among Hispanics in Springfield, Massachusetts, where I had as a partner Eloy Cruz, a Cuban American pastor from Brooklyn. All our conversations were in Spanish, using a rather different vocabulary than I had learned in the navy, but I could drive the automobile and read the scriptures. I was truly amazed at the results of Cruz's witnessing, and at the end of our week together I asked him the secret of his success. He replied, with a smile, "It is very simple. You only have to love God and the person in front of you."

These were some of the most challenging but ultimately gratifying experiences of my life, working side by side with men I had never met and on simple missions that brought what we considered to be miraculous results. My faith—in worship and in myself—was restored. This unshakable confidence was to provide me with much-needed strength and determination in later years, as my ambitions and responsibilities expanded.

AIMING FOR THE WHITE HOUSE

A FTER THE UNSUCCESSFUL 1966 governor's campaign, I finally won a fourteen-year argument and Amy came—twenty years younger than Jack. Then, with my self-confidence and trust in politics restored, I began campaigning again, this time with much more careful and thorough planning and almost four years to get acquainted with Georgia voters. I still had to earn a living, so I would stay at the warehouse with Rosalynn as late in the afternoon as possible before driving somewhere—always by myself—to speak to a civic club or some other group. I memorized as many names as I could, dictated them on the way home late at night, and the next day we would type thank-you notes on one of the earliest automatic typewriters. It used perforated tape like an old player piano, and would stop for personalizing with the insertion of individuals' names.

It was natural during these days that political discussions became increasingly important in our home, and our family thoroughly absorbed the major issues during the heated campaign of

1970. A young, handsome, and successful former governor was the leading candidate, more than equaling the combined popularity of us nine other candidates just three months before the Democratic primary. We had very little money of our own and campaign contributions were scanty, but we had a secret weapon.

While I roamed the state making speeches, planning strategy, studying issues, raising funds, and helping to manage our political organization, Rosalynn and our sons were conducting their own personal campaigns. There were few early morning factory shift lines that weren't greeted by one of them, standing patiently and handing each worker one of our pamphlets. We attended all-night sings in Waycross, stood at the entrances to circuses and county fairs, walked the coastal beaches, and all of us together surrounded the stadium when fans were entering to see the Atlanta Falcons play football. As voting time approached, Rosalynn campaigned full-time, again traveling with one of our sons and rarely in the same county where I was. Our new baby daughter, Amy, would stay with either my mother or Rosalynn's.

I remember what may have been the final turning point in the evolving personal relationship between my wife and me. At home on the weekends, I would be working on campaign tactics with our staff, calling key supporters, trying to raise money, and studying the issues. Rosalynn would have to take care of the boys, clean the house, wash clothes, cook meals, and get ready for another political foray. One Sunday afternoon I was on the telephone, and when she passed by I said, "Rosalynn, get my clothes and suitcase ready for next week."

She continued walking and replied, "Do it yourself. I have to get my own things ready."

I was startled and angry, considering her dismissive response a personal insult. But having no alternative, I was forced to accept the result of this exchange, and during the following days I was able to consider our relationship more objectively. It was obvious that my wife also considered this a seminal change, and from then on we carved out an unprecedented concept of equality and mutual respect.

Our family teamwork in the campaign paid surprisingly rich dividends. By election day, we had shaken hands with several hundred thousand people, and I was elected governor. Since then, there has been no facet of our business, personal, or political lives that we haven't shared on a relatively equal basis. I have to admit, though, that on occasion, I long for the earlier days.

JUST FIVE YEARS LATER we were embroiled in the larger and much more challenging campaign for president, but some of the factors were unchanged. Once again, I was relatively unknown, we had little money, and most of the historically involved political activists were committed to other candidates. I remember that there was a nationwide Gallup poll the day after I announced my candidacy that asked potential voters to state their preference for the next Democratic nominee. Thirty-two names were proposed, including well-known senators and congressmen, a few governors, Walter Cronkite, Julian Bond (not old enough to be president), and even George Gallup, Jr. I was distressed when I couldn't find my name on the list, but we planned our strategy carefully and once again decided to launch our proven secret weapon.

While many of my opponents were involved in their daily duties in state houses or the U.S. Congress, we Carters had seven simultaneous campaigns under way, usually each in a different state. Most often with no staff person accompanying them, my mother, her younger sister Emily, Rosalynn, our oldest son, Jack, and his wife, Judy, our second son, Chip, and his wife, Caron, and our youngest son, Jeff, and his wife, Annette, represented me wherever they were. Rosalynn's mother kept our daughter during the campaign.

On Saturday afternoons we would all assemble in our home in Plains for several hours of reporting our experiences to one another. We needed to know the questions, concerns, recommendations, and criticisms of farmers in Nebraska, schoolteachers in Wisconsin, loggers in Oregon, ranchers in Wyoming, fishermen in Maine, and steelworkers in Pennsylvania. We brought lists of newly pledged supporters, cash contributions, and names of volunteers who were willing to work full-time.

We shared notes to be certain that we were preaching the same sermon on gun control, abortion, welfare benefits, agricultural supplements, housing, and the federal role in education. Later in the campaign a lot of emphases shifted, to nuclear weaponry, the Middle East peace process, the relationship between China and Taiwan, and immigration. A committee of key policy advisers working in Atlanta submitted written issue papers to me, and all of us strove to follow them precisely after they were approved. The news media were concentrating on our truthfulness and consistency, so with an extremely sensitive issue like abortion it was necessary to use exactly the same wording in our comments in a more liberal state like Massachusetts and among more conservative voters in Iowa.

After attending Sunday school and worship services, we would drive to Atlanta for an afternoon rally that grew from a few dozen to a few thousand as our political strength increased. Following reports from us, our campaign leaders, and issues analysts, we would meet with our top staff members, and all of us Carters would receive advice on itineraries for our next week's travels.

Our family members adopted a policy of never spending the night in a motel or hotel but seeking private families to be our hosts. This saved scarce campaign funds and also cemented personal relationships with people in hundreds of communities, proving to be so easy and effective that we applied the same rules to all our volunteers and paid workers. Later, we had a reception at the White House for all our family's hosts, and almost eight hundred came to let us thank them once again. We issued small brass plaques that said, "A member of Jimmy Carter's family slept here."

No one was aware of our political progress until R. W. Apple of *The New York Times* left the usual news media hangouts in the hotel bars and lobbies in Des Moines and made a personal survey through the rural areas of Iowa. A top headline the following week reported that, miraculously, I was the leading candidate in the state. Throughout 1975 I had spent weeks there, not able to gain any publicity, speaking in college classrooms and from auctioneers' stands at livestock barns, and visiting county officials, newspaper offices, and factory shift lines. It was too late for opponents to overcome my lead, and the caucus results put me in first place.

We learned what it meant to share fully in a complex and far-reaching political campaign and what a great advantage this team approach gave us over all the other candidates. All of us Carters had concentrated efforts on the first primary in New Hampshire, and hundreds of Georgia volunteers, known as the "Peanut Brigade," had joined us. I won again.

Now the other candidates began to marshal an "ABC" (Anybody but Carter) effort. In effect, they decided to withdraw from future contests all but one or two of the strongest candidates in order not to split up the ABC vote. The next major test would be in Florida, which seemed to be the best place to stop my momentum and, they hoped, end my campaign. George Wallace, the segregationist governor of Alabama, had swept Florida four years earlier and was expected to retain his previous strength. Senator Henry "Scoop" Jackson was known to be a strong champion of Israel and presumed to have a lock on the powerful Jewish organizations in Miami and other popular places for retirees.

Almost a year earlier, Rosalynn had adopted Florida as a special place to concentrate her campaign efforts, and she first drove for two weeks around the state and subsequently spent sixty-five more full days there. She spoke to Rotary and Lions Clubs, often without prior notice of her visit, walked from office to office in county courthouses, and searched for radio transmission towers so she could drop in on the local radio disc jockeys.

If they had no idea who was even running for president, she would hand them two or three written questions and say, "Just ask me these."

Primarily thanks to this all-inclusive family team effort, I became President of the United States, and the shared responsibility of the campaign itself was a challenging and gratifying experience that bound all of us into a real team. It seemed that intense competition always aroused our highest performance, closest intimacy, and greatest mutual respect.

OUTDOORS TOGETHER

WHEN I LOOK BACK over the past eighty years for times of greatest pleasure and enjoyment, it is possible to remember only a few such experiences that didn't involve other people. Reading is one exception, of course, but much of the satisfaction of these quietest of times is the later sharing of ideas and discoveries with others. This applies to almost anything I've learned from newspapers, magazines, and books, which seems to be greatly enriched when I discuss the subject with Rosalynn or one of my friends.

A more convincing exception for me is spending time in our family's fields and woodlands. I've often said that, in another life, I'd like to be a forester or a game and fish ranger. There is an almost indescribable sense of peace and pleasure when I'm alone, especially quite early in the day, and wandering over the same remote areas that I first saw as a little boy following my father.

• • •

ROSALYNN AND I STILL LIVE in Plains, Georgia, in the house that we built in 1961. There are about 630 other citizens in the town, and we have been somewhat disappointed that none of our family has decided to join us here. Our oldest son, Jack, lived in Bermuda for about seven years as a banker and has recently moved to the outskirts of Las Vegas. Fortunately, our second son, Chip, our youngest son, Jeff, and our daughter, Amy, live and work in or near Atlanta. Of our grandchildren, Hugo is still in kindergarten; Jamie, Margaret, and Jeremy are in high school; Casey is a recent high school graduate who is deciding on a next move; Sarah Rosemary, James, and Joshua are in college; Jason is practicing law; John is a film producer in Hollywood; and Sarah Elizabeth is a professional artist living in New York City. We have a very scattered and diverse family, and one of the ambitions that Rosalynn and I share is to bring them together often enough for us all to know each other.

Remembering how my father took me along, Rosalynn and I have tried to involve our own family in some of our outdoor experiences. In addition to hunting and fishing in one of the ponds on our own farmland, one of our favorite destinations is a plantation in northern Florida that is within easy driving distance of Plains. There is a superb lake there, and since all three generations of Carters are avid and competitive fishermen, this is one of our family's favorite excursions. We go to the lake at daybreak and fish all day, except breaks for meals and perhaps a brief afternoon nap. While casting for largemouth bass, we watch the circling bald eagles, ospreys, wood storks, cormorants, anhingas, and other birds, sometimes splash water toward the larger alligators to keep them away from our small boats, shout and hold up the larger fish for envious viewing, keep enough for a good meal, and release all the others for future enjoyment. One of my most gratifying moments was when I had been fishing for several hours alone with our little grandson Joshua, and he looked up at me and said, "Papá, this is the life!"

I've never seen our smaller children more excited than when hunting raccoons and opossums with me and some farmer friends who own good hunting dogs. Since it is not necessary to kill the animals, the attractiveness of this sport is tramping through deep woodlands and swamps at night and following the dogs. Each of the hounds has its own distinctive voice, and it is obvious when the pitch and intensity of these sounds change while the dogs are just searching for a scent, when they strike a trail, are on the chase, and then the excited baying when the prey is treed. When this happens, all of us move as fast as possible to the site, crashing through brush and wading streams, carrying flashlights to avoid eye-level limbs, the thickest brambles, and deep stump holes that could break a leg.

Finally under the tree, the dogs are partially constrained while we encircle the site, shining our narrowly focused beams upward until the hidden 'coon or 'possum looks down, and its brightly reflecting eyes reveal its presence and identity. At least when little children are present, this is the end of the hunt. The dogs are tethered and taken away to repeat the process, leaving the treed animal unscathed. On other occasions, the hunters might later enjoy a good South Georgia meal.

• • •

ONE OF MY LIFETIME HABITS has been scanning the ground for projectile points and other archaeological artifacts of Native Americans. Since leaving the farm, I've continued this habit even in city parks, golf courses, college campuses, and along other paths that thousands of people may use each day. In fact, I've been surprisingly successful in finding arrowheads even in these kinds of public places.

As did many farm boys, I began this hobby walking through the fields, through gullies, or alongside roadways after heavy rains had washed away the loose topsoil. The rain would expose pieces of rock or other insoluble items, and my interest would be immediately titillated when I saw pieces of flint, products of chipping this extremely hard stone into the tools used by Indians during the thousands of years before white men drove them out of Georgia. Although a stray arrowhead can be found almost anywhere, there were a few prime fields on our farm where Indian villages had been located near a stream, and pieces of broken clay pottery would always be present in the same fields.

The best time of the year for finding arrowheads was the first spring plowing after a long winter of rains, and the earth in front of my plow was never turned over without my examining it closely. This was the only competition with my father in which I could prevail, because he spent much more time supervising the complex work of the plantation than he did walking back and forth across the individual fields with a hoe, carrying a cotton sack, or behind a mule. We planted a large acreage of watermelons each year, and these were also fertile fields for artifacts. We could not plow after the long vines extended across the surface, but one of my duties was walking along the rows and cutting off the deformed or diseased melons before they could sap too much nutrient from the good ones.

Finding an especially beautiful point was a source of pride, and I was always eager to get back home and display it to my admiring parents and siblings. I had accumulated several hundred by the time I left home for college and the navy, and I added to my collection whenever possible.

Our entire family lived in Atlanta while I was governor (the best political job I ever had), and I always yearned to leave the big city and return to our rural area, even for a day or two at a time. I would visit first the warehouse and the farms to assess what was happening with our business, but I was also looking for additional ways for Rosalynn and the boys to be involved in some of my outdoor experiences. One afternoon, I thought about the possibility of their joining me in walking through some of my favorite arrowhead fields and was delighted when they took up my earliest hobby. From then on, we would line up abreast about ten or twelve feet apart and walk back and forth, covering even a large field in a few hours. We tried to scan every square inch as we moved slowly, stopping whenever one saw a promising piece of flint.

The overwhelming majority of sightings proved to be chips that were just by-products from ancient craftsmen, nicely shaped water oak leaves, or large rocks with an interesting portion exposed. We became rather competitive in these efforts, and a good find always brought some brief congratulations, only partially concealing envy. We put a small marking code on each artifact, identifying the finder and the location. On our most productive day, in our favorite field, we found twenty-six unbroken arrowheads.

A few years ago some experienced archaeologists took about fifteen hundred of our best pieces and categorized each by style, likely Indian tribe, probable use, and age. They were able to make an accurate analysis because I had taken care not to dilute the collection with artifacts from distant places. My most persistent dream, even during recent years, has been of finding a place almost covered with beautiful artifacts. There is something fascinating about these highly diverse mementos of the former inhabitants of the land we now claim as our own, and our family would often have an extensive debate about the tribal identity of a point's last user and the circumstances under which it may have been lost. I wrote a poem about this topic.

THE HISTORY OF A POINT

Walking through a fallow field,
I found an arrowhead
More lovely than I'd ever seen,
Up on an earthen pedestal
Not packed by rain
But sheltered by the point itself.
Caressing it, I let my mind race back to when
A chief's son wore it as a charm,
But somehow lost it and then feared
Calamities would come;
Or when, nowhere near this place,

A hunter made a shot, close-up,
Sure his matchless arrow would not miss,
But then the deer escaped,
Later to reach here, and to die;
Or when, in war, it struck a brave
Who pushed it through to save his life
But never saw it, hidden in his blood;
Or perhaps this arrowhead
Had such a beauty it was buried
With the artist who had shaped it.
Or none of these.
Without a trace of mood or hone
The point seems always to have lain alone.

I'VE ALWAYS BEEN A HUNTER and fisherman, and my interests began with harvesting family meals by catching fish from nearby creeks and shooting squirrels and rabbits. Later, I adopted the more adult challenges of doves, quail, and ducks, all of which have been plentiful on our own land. I never saw either a wild turkey or a deer in those early days; they had been decimated after the Indians were driven from their native hunting lands. I am proud that I was able to play a role as governor and outdoorsman in promoting their reintroduction and increase in all areas of our state. Because of their enlightened protection by hunters, both species are now plentiful once again. Although I've never chosen to hunt deer, I lease hunting rights on our farmland to others, who are encouraged by game biologists to harvest a substantial number each year to prevent overpopulation.

For the past quarter century, I have been an avid but restrained turkey hunter. During Georgia's relatively brief spring season, I take advantage of every opportunity to be out each morning about an hour before sunrise. Completely camouflaged, I enter the forest as quietly as possible and immerse myself in the surrounding environment. I first hear whip-poor-wills and chuck-will's-widows calling as dawn approaches, then the twittering of various songbirds and the distant song of mourning doves and barred owls, and finally the raucous cries of common crows. If a gobbler doesn't waken to this disturbing sound, I may imitate the crows more loudly to precipitate a response from a nearby still-roosting gobbler. Then comes the enticement of the male by my imitation of a turkey hen. If unsuccessful at the first location, I wander through the woodlands for a few miles, pausing every now and then to try another call.

The legal limit in Georgia is three gobblers (and no hens), but I've always been satisfied with one for Thanksgiving and another for Christmas dinner. I sometimes reach this goal early in the season, and still go out each morning with a camera instead of a gun. Through books, conversations with other hunters, and my own experiences, I have learned a lot about turkeys and also about our own more remote and inaccessible swamps and wooded areas, which I would otherwise seldom or never see. I've tested and developed my own woodland skills, my visual acuity, and much-needed patience, and have acknowledged my innumerable mistakes as I tested wits with this extremely wary and intelligent bird.

I considered these solitary excursions to be perfectly idyllic until one morning I induced Rosalynn to go with me. The pleasures were greatly magnified as she would sit beside a large tree, surrounded by a camouflaged netting that permitted her to see and not be seen, while I positioned myself nearby. Sometimes a coyote, red fox, or raccoon would wander by, a cautious deer would approach from upwind to within a few yards, or a large and brilliant pileated woodpecker would perch overhead and explore for its breakfast in a dead limb with its powerful hammering beak.

Rosalynn has shared my excitement as the battle of wits with elusive turkeys evolved, and she often interrupts my later accounts of a few successes and many failures with her own recollections. In performing our routine duties as caretakers of the family farmlands, Rosalynn is now a much more able partner in understanding when to thin overcrowded trees, detecting beetle infestations early, and deciding when to harvest and replant a mature section of our woodlands. She has learned how to read a topographical map, how to utilize deer paths to navigate through thickets, how to employ the sun, moon, or a compass to avoid being lost, and how to identify different species of trees.

There is a special pleasure in sharing experiences with my family on the same land that I enjoyed more than a half century ago with my father and black playmates, and that our ancestors have known for seven generations.

CHALLENGING SPORTS

ROSALYNN AND I STUDIED in the same classrooms, played varsity basketball on the same court, swam in the same pool, and learned to dance in the same pavilion, but we were separated by too many years to participate with each other. I was a tennis player and a long-distance runner, but it was not until we had been married twenty-five years that I considered reaching out to Rosalynn to join me in these active sports I had learned to cherish from my boyhood.

Rosalynn had always been a good athlete, and she began jogging with me during the years when I was governor. The mansion was in an eighteen-acre enclosure (the same as the White House), and we had a roadway that went up and down a fairly steep hill. Beginning with a half mile or so, we gradually extended our distance together to several miles. Much later, when we started traveling to other nations on projects of The Carter Center, this was a wonderful way to gain unique insight into people's lives in capital cities and the countrysides. We have visited many nations, and the normal temptation for us as American visitors is to stay in a Western-style hotel, perhaps swim in the pool, meet with political leaders or specialists in a subject, and then leave the country without any involvement in the local community.

Instead, we have habitually gotten up early, donned our running shoes, and jogged through the most interesting parts of the town long before the traffic builds up to pollute the air and when housewives and shopkeepers are preparing for the day's activities. It is surprising how different are the main business districts or historic areas of Stockholm, Tokyo, Beijing, Cairo, Casablanca, Caracas, Tirana, Cotonou, Buenos Aires, Jakarta, San Francisco, Bangkok—or New York—just after daybreak and before sunrise. Everything is quiet, few vehicles are on the streets, people are sweeping the sidewalks, placing decorative flowers in front of their houses or businesses, and grocers are stacking up pineapples, oranges, cassava, or guava. In China and other Eastern countries, hundreds of people, especially the elderly, are quietly engaged in tai chi exercises, and cages occupied by tiny birds are being aired by their proud owners.

Rosalynn and I had perhaps our most interesting early morning excursions in the Middle East during the mid-1980s. One year, after President Anwar Sadat was assassinated, President Mubarak reissued a long-standing invitation for us to travel up the Nile River as guests of his government. Each morning we would leave our small excursion ship and run perpendicular to the river out into the surrounding villages. When near one of the famous archaeological sites, we could jog in and out of the ancient places when no one else was there except perhaps a lonely security guard.

In Israel, we told Jerusalem's mayor, Teddy Kollek, how much we had enjoyed running around the outside of the Old City several times on different visits, and he asked if we'd like to be the first people to have a new experience. The next morning we went up to the top of the high stone wall that surrounds the holy places and jogged around its periphery as far as possible in each direction. The large stone surface was extremely uneven, so we moved carefully and stopped to absorb the incredibly impressive sight when the sun rose slowly over the Dome of the Rock and the eastern horizon.

We also visited Syria, Lebanon, Jordan, and Saudi Arabia every couple of years during that time and were always welcomed to take our early morning exercise. We never felt threatened or even uncomfortable because we were always greeted with smiles and friendship. Under a dictatorial regime, with soldiers ever alert for disturbances, the streets seemed safest.

Our most dangerous moment was on a trip in a friend's airplane to inspect Carter Center projects in Africa. After landing at night to refuel in the Azores, we obtained permission from the control tower to get some exercise by running down the runway and back, with a vehicle following about seventy-five yards behind us so its headlights could help us see irregularities in the surface. All of a sudden, we heard a voice from out in the weeds shout, "Halt!" Confused, we ran a few steps further. The command was repeated, and we heard the unmistakable sound of a weapon being cocked. Now perfectly still, we raised our hands as high as possible and faced the dedicated soldier, who was intent on protecting the airport from unauthorized intruders. The automobile swerved right and let its light beam illuminate the scene of the guard standing there with his finger on the trigger of an automatic rifle aimed directly at my chest. We later learned that the control tower had sent out a radio message about our running, but this soldier had had his receiver turned off to save the battery.

ONE OF THE MOST CHALLENGING new sports that Rosalynn and I have taken up is downhill skiing. One of our friends from the White House was from New Mexico, and he arranged accommodations for our family at a winter resort in Taos. Since I was sixty-two and Rosalynn three years younger, we made it clear to everyone that rather than break our necks on a ski slope, we planned to stay in the lodge, read, and do some writing.

We were sitting around the fire on our first night there, and not surprisingly, the subject was about finally becoming old. I still remember some of the attempts at humor:

"Anybody who can still do at sixty what he was doing at twenty wasn't doing much at twenty."

"Mountain climbers climb mountains for the same reason I go around them. They are there."

"When you're pushing sixty, that's exercise enough."

"You know you're old when your children are the same age as you are."

Finally, one of the young grandchildren said, "Papá, you're old when you don't have to keep up with us any longer."

Needless to say, the next morning we were taking lessons,

and we learned only later that our chosen resort was one of the most difficult in the Rockies for beginners. We made enough progress to try again the following winter, this time in Crested Butte, Colorado, and for a dozen seasons we returned there. Even the smallest grandchildren, as soon as they shed their diapers, have become good skiers.

I was determined to stay up with them on the slopes and did so until the winter of 1994, when I severely wrenched my left knee while trying to make a rapid turn in deep powder. For seven years after that, for skiing, tennis, or other sports, I had to wear a "Joe Namath" steel brace that prevented any possible twisting of my leg. Rosalynn was pleased when we decided to limit our runs to the green and blue slopes, no longer attempting to compete with the younger folks on the blacks and even more challenging runs.

We often made a second winter ski trip to the Aspen area and were invited to stay in the large ski lodge of Saudi Arabian Prince Bandar, who represents his country as ambassador in Washington. On a mountain overlooking Aspen's four ski areas, the place was like heaven for our grandchildren. In addition to superb service from a staff of skilled servants, fine food, and luxurious accommodations, there was an indoor swimming pool and a large recreation room with the most advanced holographic video games.

One of our natural motivations as grandparents is to cement ties of love and appreciation with the younger children, so it is always a cherished moment when one of them lets us know their sentimental feelings toward us. One morning at breakfast, our grandson Jeremy looked across at me and called out, "Papá!"

I replied, "What is it, Jeremy?"

"Can I ask you a question?"

"Yes, of course." He was just big enough to see over the edge of the table, and I expected some question about how soon we would be leaving for the ski slopes.

He hesitated a few moments and then asked, "Papá, are you going to die?"

I was really touched by his concern and replied, "Yes, sweet boy. Everyone will die someday, but I hope it won't be any time soon."

There was a long silence around the table, and finally I asked, "Jeremy, why did you ask me about dying?"

"When you die, can we still come to Bandar's place to ski?"

WHITE HOUSE VACATIONS

OR AN INCUMBENT PRESIDENT, enjoyment is not in doing exotic and exciting things that may be available only to famous people or affluent tourists. Pleasure comes in being away from the news media and the pressing duties of public service, if possible in relative solitude with one's family or close friends. Our striving to achieve this goal was not always successful, but we managed at least to have a relatively normal family life even while in the White House.

Amy was just three years old when I became governor, and six years older when we moved to Washington. Jack had finished his three years of military service in Vietnam and then acquired a degree in nuclear physics and a law degree. After the campaign, he, his wife, and son, Jason, moved back to Georgia. Our second son, Chip, remained interested in political affairs, worked in the Democratic Party, and represented our family in a multitude of official and unofficial events that typically help to fill the life of a first family. Chip and his wife lived in the White House with us, and their son, James, was born just a month after I was inaugurated. Jeff was still a college student and transferred to George Washington University, where he studied geography and computer science, so it was natural for him and his wife, Annette, to join us in the White House as well.

It would be difficult to exaggerate how lively were our discussions at suppertime about the political interrelationships in which each of us was involved. Amy pitched in with her views of the public school system in the District of Columbia and the lives of her classmates, many of them children of the servants in foreign embassies. The older boys had their own interests and perspectives in college and at work, and Rosalynn was deeply committed to mental health issues and, except for those involving military secrets, kept abreast of all the public affairs in which I was involved. I learned that people who had criticisms or complaints were much more likely to express them to my family than to me, while Rosalynn and the children relished the opportunity to relay them. All of us really enjoyed these years together.

I was determined to reduce unnecessary expenditures in the federal budget, but after our first visit to Camp David, I told my budget director never to inform me what it cost or to suggest that its services be reduced in any way. As other modern presidents have learned as well, one of the most delightful surprises of the office is this presidential retreat, about a thirty-five-minute helicopter flight from the south lawn of the White House. The 125-acre resort in Maryland's Catoctin Mountain Park was established by President Franklin Roosevelt in 1942 and later named by President Eisenhower for his grandson. The amenities at Camp David are the same as at the White House, with a global communications center, comfortable quarters, swimming pool, tennis court, and bowling alley. We were always eager to enjoy its seclusion and beauty. Although my cabinet and staff members had the same access to me at Camp David as in the White House, they were all very reluctant to call me when they knew I was attempting to relax. There was also a small but well-stocked trout stream at the base of the mountain, and we often biked both within and outside the tightly secured compound.

The winters offered the most distinctive differences, with much more snow on the mountain than in Washington, so we enjoyed our first experience with cross-country skiing within the presidential retreat and along the hiking and equestrian trails in nearby state parks. We also had sleds and snowmobiles that we used on the steep slopes within the camp.

Our most frightening experience was when we were pulling one-year-old James around on a sled, stopped for a brief conversation, and then looked to see him moving at a faster and faster pace away from us. I chased him through the deep snow and finally saw him and the sled disappear over a ten-foot cliff into a thick forest. When I finally arrived, with my heart pounding, I found the sled overturned and James sitting in the snow laughing.

Another mishap had a less joyful ending. I was skiing down a steep slope near our cottage on very thin snow, hit an exposed rock, and broke my left clavicle just two weeks before my term as president expired. We had a going-away reception for the fourteen hundred White House employees, and despite the tight strapping, I could feel the bones grinding together every time I shook hands in the interminable receiving line.

Almost twenty years later, President Bill Clinton came to The Carter Center to award the Presidential Medal of Freedom to Rosalynn and me, and he was surrounded by our young grandchildren during a quiet moment. Soon they and the president were posing together for photographs, all of them wearing dark glasses like the Blues Brothers. When they told him they had never seen the White House or Camp David, he arranged for us to make a one-night visit to each place. It was a real delight for all of us older Carters to serve as guides to the young kids and some newly acquired in-laws.

WHILE SERVING IN WASHINGTON, we had contemplated returning to Plains as frequently as possible, as we had done while I was governor, but we ran into problems. On our first visit, we flew to the air force base at Warner Robins and drove the ninety miles to Plains. It required almost every state patrolman in Georgia to manage traffic, including blocking all the side roads that intersected our route. When we arrived in Plains, the little town was packed with friends and supporters, curiosity seekers, and representatives of dozens of special interest groups who wanted to make an appeal to me or just to be photographed waving their placards in front of the dozens of television cameras that always follow a president. It was almost impossible for us to walk down the town's only sidewalk to visit our old friends and neighbors, so we were largely confined to the secured area around our home.

I decided to go to a remote part of our farm to hunt quail with the White House physician, Bill Lukash, and two of my bird dogs. A horde of news reporters followed our car, and I asked the Secret Service to block the small field road so we could walk through my fields with some privacy. When we returned to the main road a few hours later, the reporters shouted, "Did you get any quail?" I held up seven fingers, said "Enough for supper," and the success of our hunt was immediately transmitted around the world as the top news story of the day. The following Sunday, back in Washington, there were hundreds of raucous demonstrators in front of First Baptist Church when our family went to worship, accusing me of being a murderer.

At a family conference in the White House we all decided that, despite our love for Plains, it was counterproductive for us to seek any kind of relaxation or normality there. We would still make a few visits home, including each celebration of Christmas, but we needed another destination if we wanted to go to Georgia. As governor, I had acquired as many of our coastal islands as possible, so that they could be preserved in their natural state and made available for a limited number of visitors. Sapelo Island was my first choice as a presidential refuge, since there was a beautiful mansion there, built in the 1930s by the Reynolds tobacco family and adequate to accommodate our entire family. One of the most attractive features of these visits was a small group of black families who lived at Hog Hammock. They were descendants of liberated slaves who had worked on the rice plantations, spoke with a strong Gullah accent, and maintained a tenuous connection by boat with the mainland. Surrounding this small inhabited area were fifteen thousand acres of undeveloped beaches, marshlands, and forests of palmettos, ancient pines, and live oaks.

We strictly limited the size of our presidential entourage, excluded all news media except for one brief interview, and made careful arrangements with the Hog Hammock leaders for us to live alongside them and worship in their tiny church at Raccoon Bluff. We also joined them on occasion for feasts of oysters, mullet, or pork barbecue, all plentifully available from the tidal streams and the overpopulation of wild hogs on the island. Our only needs from the civilized world were an elaborate communi cations system and a few Jeeps that we adults could use to reach the more distant parts of the island for fishing, exploring, and swimming during the warmer months. There was one that was set aside for me, labeled "Jeep One," which some of the rangers joked was a sacrificial vehicle because of my limited recent practice as a driver. During colder days, all of us enjoyed a large and ornately decorated pool inside the mansion.

BESIDES CAMP DAVID, Plains, Sapelo Island, and official visits to foreign nations, we attempted to find other places to enjoy together. In 1978, after a year of effort, I had finally arranged for President Anwar Sadat and Prime Minister Menachem Begin to join me at Camp David for peace talks. Having wrestled for months with this crucial issue and a multitude of others, I felt a need to get away and relax for a few days. Secretary of the Interior Cecil Andrus had been governor of Idaho, and he suggested that our family join him for a raft trip down the Middle Fork of the Salmon River (also called the River of No Return).

This is truly a wilderness area, with the precipitous banks of the stream almost completely inaccessible except by helicopter. There had to be radio transmitter stations established at strategic points by the White House communications specialists, but otherwise Cecil, Rosalynn, Jack, Chip, Amy, and I assumed the roles of typical adventurous tourists and entered the deep canyon on large rubber rafts. Our family was in one raft and Secretary Andrus and some of our necessary staff members in the other. We were all holding on for life during the more steep and powerful rapids and casting flies in the more placid stretches of the stream, with the usual excited competition between us. Each group would catch and release about fifty trout every day, and then the victors would chortle during our stops along the shore to eat or sleep.

Our guides managed the rafts with huge oars called "sweeps," which permitted some steerage through the rapids and propulsion in the slow-moving intervals of calm water. Our sweep broke in half as we were going through the most formidable rapid, and the guides said we would have to wait for a half day or so for another to be brought to the river. Instead, Jack and I used our marlinespike seamanship skills from the navy and lashed the two pieces together strongly enough to survive the remainder of our voyage. An assembly of news media were waiting when we disembarked at the end of our expedition and asked the inevitable question: "How did the family like the boat trip?"

There was a chorus of responses: "The best three days of our lives!"

From the river we went to a lodge in the Grand Teton National Park, where we jogged, went sightseeing, fished, and sailed. Rosalynn and I had fly-casting lessons from Don Daughenbaugh, who left his regular duties as a high school teacher in Pennsylvania each year to serve as a Yellowstone Park ranger during the summer months.

Fishing one morning in a swift current of the nearby Snake River with one of my favorite dry flies, named "Irresistible," I had a vicious strike. I pulled back strongly on the rod, and in an instant the hook was embedded in my right cheek. Fortunately, my companion was the physician Bill Lukash, who had learned from other fly-fishermen how to treat this emergency. While I lay on my back in the shoreline grass, thankful that we had excluded television cameras from our outing, he inserted a strong line through the curve of the hook, held down the eye in which the leader was tied, and snatched out the barb through its entry channel.

My presidential duties intruded even into this remote vacation spot. In addition to staying in touch with the vice president and other leaders, I spent several hours each day studying two voluminous briefing books that were designed to let me know how and why the two adversaries might react to all the potential issues they would have to face at Camp David within the next week. This information was extremely complex, of course, but one tidbit would prove to be very significant and would make success possible. Under pressure, Sadat would likely resort to generalities, including geopolitical concepts and regional inter-relationships. He was almost impervious to the domestic politics of Egypt. In contrast, Begin was expected to turn to minutiae, semantics, the internal politics of his own Likud Party, and would have little concern about broader international issues.

This family jaunt was an unforgettable lesson in the advantages of combining business with pleasure. Completely relaxed after our outdoor adventures, my mind seemed to be remarkably clear, and I read the briefing books as though they were vivid historical novels. What I absorbed in advance of the peace talks helped ensure that the thirteen days of negotiation would be successful.

EVEN DURING THE INTENSE and often unpleasant Camp David negotiations, I realized that all three of us leaders needed a brief time of relaxation, so I planned a visit to nearby Gettysburg. It was a Sunday afternoon, and I sat between Sadat and Begin in the limousine and informed them that we would not have any discussion of current events. Sadat, the Egyptian and Israeli generals, and I were quite familiar with what had happened at the Civil War site, all of us having studied the battle in our various military schools. I was somewhat concerned because Begin was excluded completely from the excited discussions. However, when we arrived at the location of Lincoln's Address, all of us stood mute for a few seconds, and then Begin quietly recited every word of the historic speech. We drove back with a clearer realization of our differences but with enhanced mutual respect. There had been a few moments of remarkable sharing.

FLY-FISHING

A S I WRITE THIS CHAPTER, I am at one of my favorite places on earth, alongside Spruce Creek in Pennsylvania, a stream that rises from deep springs, meanders about thirteen miles through meadows between mountain ridges, and joins the Juniata River six miles below my vantage point. Our family is staying in a cottage that we have visited for twenty-five years, missing only one fly-fishing season, when I had rotator cuff surgery on my right arm. There is a small waterfall burbling in front of me with a long pool just above, and the far bank of the stream is covered by overhanging hemlocks.

A trout rises to take a mayfly under this protective cover every minute or two, and during certain predictable days of the year, thousands of the beautiful insects leave the bottom of the stream, where they have spent either one or two years in the nymphal stage, rise to the surface, quickly sprout wings, and fly up into surrounding trees. After their wings dry, they can be seen in the air performing their mating dance and, after breeding, the females alight on the water to restart the perennial cycle by laying their eggs before dying. At these times, the pool is literally covered by circles as fish rise to gorge themselves on the insects and perhaps take a skillfully tied artificial one, to be brought in to a fisherman and then carefully released.

Around a bend up the creek is a higher waterfall, larger pools, and a covered bridge. On one of our summer fishing trips, Rosalynn and I drove up from Plains to help build it, and a plaque on a large white stone, dated May 26, 1989, commemorates this event. Yesterday morning as I left the front porch, walked along the stream, and approached the bridge, I confronted a large black bear that looked at me for a few seconds, then slowly turned and meandered up the high mountain ridge that overlooks the meadow. There is a hillside visible further upstream on which Holstein dairy cows graze, and each afternoon we have watched a large turkey gobbler strut before the admiring eyes of three hens. For the past three days they have appeared at almost exactly 4:30 P.M. for this mating ritual, disappearing into the mountain woodland before sundown.

Wayne Harpster and his family are the stewards of this domain, having lived alongside Spruce Creek for almost sixty years, since Wayne was a seven-year-old. About halfway from our cottage and the origin of Spruce Creek, located well back from the stream to preserve its pristine character, is one of the finest dairies in the world. The three Harpster sons help to cultivate and harvest about three thousand acres of corn and alfalfa that produce silage, as the prime feed for the eighteen hundred superb cows that are milked three times a day. To prevent erosion, the fields are planted without having been tilled during the past two decades. Wayne realizes that a portion of the forage crop is always harvested by white-tailed deer, and in late afternoon tours in a four-wheeler we can often see as many as two hundred deer grazing in the fields.

All three generations of the Harpsters and the Carters are friends, and we have shared a number of delightful experiences in addition to our annual visits, including trips to several other nations. We first met Wayne and his family while I was president, and the Yellowstone Park ranger Don Daughenbaugh recommended a place close enough to Washington to go fishing on the weekends. We managed to develop one of the best kept secrets of my time in the White House.

As early as possible on Friday afternoons we would fly to Camp David, where several dozen news reporters always assembled to watch us disembark from Marine One. While they retired to a nearby motel to spend the weekend, we would go to our cabin, change clothes, get our fly rods, and then helicopter another half hour or so before landing in the well-concealed Harpsters' meadow within sight of where I'm sitting this morning. On Sunday afternoons, we would reverse the flight schedule and return to Washington.

Since Rosalynn and I had grown up in the South, with water too warm for trout, our fishing was always for bream, bass, catfish, and other species that can be caught with a fly rod but usually with a cane pole or spinning tackle. It was not until we moved to the governor's mansion in Atlanta that we had easy access to the Chattahoochee River, where the water runs cold from the bottom of Buford Dam and where brown and rainbow trout flourish. One of my earliest ambitions as Georgia's chief executive was to learn this new sport, and I was soon in the river with Georgia's game and fish director, Jack Crockford, casting awkwardly from inside an inner tube as we floated down the frigid stream. I caught a number of fish during those four years but never attempted to master the finer techniques of an angler until, as president, I began making these visits to Pennsylvania.

Keeping our secret, some of America's foremost experts on making rods, casting, tying flies, stream management, entomology, and the finer aspects of fishing technique would meet us at Spruce Creek (and once at Camp David) to share some of their skills. By then, I had become familiar with the writings of some of these masters and knew how to cast a line, study currents in a stream, and control the movement of a dry fly as it floated naturally and without the line dragging it in an irregular way that was alarming to waiting trout.

My attempts to arouse Rosalynn's interest in fly-fishing had been unsuccessful until we took the float trip down the Middle Fork of the Salmon River and spent a few days on the lake near the Grand Tetons, where she was introduced to a fly rod and reel. Rosalynn later practiced for hours, casting into the swimming pool at Camp David. She had a natural talent and soon developed precise control and proper placement of the fly.

I set up a fly-tying desk in what we called Harry Truman's study, in the second-floor room adjacent to our White House bedroom, and would spend hours at a time producing some of my favorite patterns while listening to music ranging from Willie Nelson to Leontyne Price. Like building furniture or painting a picture, the development of this art would create a separate and relaxing world for me.

Now, in addition to our annual visits to Spruce Creek, Rosalynn and I make two or three excursions to other trout streams each year, both in our own country—in the Rockies, the Northwest, and Alaska—and abroad. We've fished in Finland, Switzerland, England, Wales, Ireland, New Zealand, Japan, Russia, and several times in Canada. One of our most delightful fishing trips was with our entire family camping alongside Slough Creek in Yellowstone National Park to fish for cutthroat trout.

Fly-fishing has evolved into a pastime that we will be able to share for many years and has introduced us to a wide circle of friends whom we would never otherwise have known, and it was inevitable that we introduce our children and grandchildren to the sport. The term "natural beauty" is almost superfluous in describing a trout stream, because these delicate creatures inhabit only the waters that are pure and cold, most often originating from deep and bubbling springs or from those that descend remote and unpolluted mountainsides. Fly-fishers are extremely protective of the fish, the pristine water, and the surroundings, and pride themselves on honoring all the protocols and customs that have developed during several centuries. We have been thrilled to take our place among these practitioners of the art.

TOURISTS IN CHINA AND JAPAN

P RESIDENT RICHARD NIXON made his historic visit to the People's Republic of China in February 1972 and declared, "There is only one China." However, he refused to say which one. There was an extremely powerful Taiwan lobby, centered in the most conservative wing of the Republican Party, which continued to insist that the only recognized government of China was in Taipei and not Beijing. The two most influential Republican leaders, President Gerald Ford and his challenger, California Governor Ronald Reagan, competed to see who could be the strongest proponent of Taiwan.

I had visited China for several weeks as a young submarine officer in 1949, just as Mao Zedong's Red Army was closing in on the last remnants of the Kuomintang's nationalist forces, and had remained fascinated with the China-Taiwan issue. As president, I decided to normalize diplomatic relations with Mainland China, and after a year of secret negotiations with Vice Premier Deng Xiaoping, made this official decision at the beginning of 1979. Almost immediately, Deng came to visit me in Washington and to make a brief tour of the United States. He insisted that I make a reciprocal visit to China, but I took no foreign trips during my last year in office because of the hostage crisis in Iran.

The Chinese invitation was reissued after I left the White House, with a special embellishment: Rosalynn and I could bring as many as six guests, and all of us would be treated as especially honored visitors, free to travel throughout the country after a few days of official ceremonies in Beijing. On our Chinese credentials, everyone had an identification: president, first lady, president's son Chip, and daughter, Amy, White House Press Secretary Jody Powell, the *Atlanta Constitution* editor Hal Gulliver, White House Appointments Secretary Phil Wise, and Wayne Harpster, world's greatest fisherman! At every official event, these titles were loudly proclaimed.

This had not been a happy time for us. Following my loss of the 1980 reelection campaign, we discovered that we were deeply in debt and worked almost without ceasing to review official records and personal diary notes in order to complete my presidential memoir to be published before Christmas. We decided to leave all our cares behind, to take full advantage of Chinese hospitality, and then to visit Japan for a few days on the way home.

In Beijing, we found that China was still a relatively closed society, with the Communist Party in full control, no free enterprise permitted, citizens restricted in their movements, and a basic uniformity of dress that was relatively unchanged since Mao and the Revolution. There were few automobiles, with almost all transportation on foot or on bicycles. In our beautiful

guesthouse we found that there were only two television chan-
nels available, and one of them was devoted almost full-time to
recounting my normalizing diplomatic relations and reviewing
every aspect of Deng's visit to the United States. Every scene in
which he and I were involved was replayed over and over. Asked
if we had any special requests, we decided to ask for bicycles so
that we could get some exercise and perhaps tour the city.

The following morning Rosalynn and I went out and found
bikes, plus a large entourage of Chinese security men com-
manded by an army colonel. He unfolded a map and began to
show me a route along which we would be permitted to travel,
saying that it had been thoroughly secured. I told him I wanted
to choose my own itinerary, and we argued back and forth until
I finally told him to call Vice Premier Deng Xiaoping and ask
him if I could bike where I wished or just where the colonel preferred. After a brief consultation with his aides, the colonel said
that a decision had been made that I could travel wherever I
wished, and there was no need for him to disturb the vice premier. That was the last effort to restrict our movements, and all
our Chinese hosts seemed dedicated to showing us the finest
aspects of their personal hospitality and the attractions of their
nation.

During my long conversations with Deng, both in Washington and during our visit to China, he was fascinated with the results of his first experiment with free enterprise for any citizens
of the People's Republic. He made it clear to me that he would
never launch crash programs in either political or economic re-
form but would first move carefully and incrementally on the

economic front, beginning with farm families. Knowing that I was a farmer, he described in detail how radical had been the transformation in Chinese farmers' lives and was very eager for me to visit some of these farmers. He laughed as he said, "I have observed quite a difference. A farmer will stay up all night with his own sick pig but not with one that belongs to the cooperative."

His only real request, therefore, was that we fly to a northern province to observe his new system. The large agricultural cooperatives would retain 85 percent of the land, and individual farmers could have the other acreage for their own families' use. The individuals' land was always the marginal land under trees, in ditches, or on the eroded places. However, these areas quickly became the most productive. In addition, these fortunate entrepreneurs could also have one small enterprise, such as making clay pots, repairing bicycles, forging horseshoes or hammered nails, or raising up to five pigs, goats, sheep, or a small flock of chickens or ducks. One of the farmers we visited was raising mink and told us that many others shared that project.

It was a wonderful experience for us to immerse ourselves in the farmers' lives, and to experience their excitement and delight with this change in their personal freedom. None of them knew that the basic plan was to extend free enterprise next to the villagers, then to family shops and other small businesses in cities, and ultimately to transform the entire nation. In effect, this would spell the end of pure communism in the People's Republic of China, and Deng told me in one of our private discussions that within a year he would authorize direct democratic elections in their 800,000 small villages. It was nice for our group to have a good time and also be involved in historic change.

We were entertained lavishly in every large city, usually with twenty-course dinners and repeated toasts, often with the formidable mao-tai, which tastes like a mixture of gin and kerosene. We had decided at least to try everything on the menu, so we experienced the widest possible diversity of exotic Oriental foods, including bird's nest soup, thousand-year-old eggs, stinky tofu, sea slugs, and other unidentifiable dishes. We always had the finest entertainment, and the tables were decorated with great dragons and other figures carved from ice, melons, or various vegetables and fruits. It seemed that national officers, governors, mayors, and other notables had free rein in ensuring that we and they enjoyed the festivities to the utmost. Almost invariably, we found ourselves singing and joining in dances around the big round tables. At Deng's direction, political speeches were kept to a minimum, and the only really formal dinner on our trip was in the Japanese Imperial Palace with Emperor Hirohito and his family.

One evening, before an extended supper, someone asked Wayne Harpster what he had been doing that day, and he replied, "Well, I've been eating and drinking for seven hours, and I also visited a Chinese dairy."

As we traveled to different provinces, we stayed in the best guesthouses, and bicycles were always waiting for our unimpeded sightseeing. It seemed that everyone knew about us and our visit, so we were welcomed into private homes and entertained in a surprisingly natural way. Even if the poorest of families could offer us only a cup of hot water or a small piece of apple, they did this with pride and without apology. At one place we went fishing for carp, and our hosts insisted on taking one of my catches and preparing it for our meal. The recipe was to poach the fish in heavily spiced milk. With a heroic effort, we consumed it all. Perhaps our most memorable tourist adventure was to receive a preview at Xi'an of the hundreds of recently discovered life-size clay figures, along with other remarkable artifacts that had been excavated but never shown to anyone other than Chinese archaeologists.

After China, we spent a few days traveling in Japan, again with an emphasis on fun. Whenever possible we stayed in Eastern-style hotels, with their sunken wooden bathtubs, sleeping mats on the floor, and foot-high tables. By this time we were all proficient with chopsticks. Knowing that Rosalynn and I were avid fly-fishers, and seeing Harpster's designation as the world's greatest fisherman, our hosts invited us to go to a stream about a third of the way up Mount Fuji. When we arrived at the hotel, some of our Japanese friends, including some notable fishermen, were to join us for supper, and we agreed to dress in traditional attire.

A Japanese lady came to our room and gave Rosalynn and me careful instructions on how to don the kimono and tie the sash. When she went to Wayne's room, he refused to let her see him seminude and insisted on dressing himself. Later, as we all proceeded to the dining area, the many bowing women and other bystanders along our path were convulsed with laughter, which they attempted unsuccessfully to conceal. It turned out there is a strict code in which the right side of the kimono is to be put against one's body and the left side then overlaps. Wayne's was backward—an arrangement reserved for corpses!

We spent a good portion of the meal that evening negotiating an international wager about whose fishing champion would prevail the following day and finally had about a hundred dollars bet on each side. The bet was publicized, and the next morning we found the perfectly clear stream heavily stocked with rainbow and brown trout but with dozens of news reporters and more than a thousand spectators crowding both banks and filling a crossing bridge. I refused to cast a fly until the people moved back to give Rosalynn and me some room and the fish an opportunity to relax. Each of my casts was televised, with special focus on any tangled lines or flies caught in nearby shrubbery. Despite this attention, each of us caught and released several trout, and Wayne was able to demonstrate his inimitable skills, catching more fish than all his Japanese competitors combined. There was a jovial ceremony when the bets were settled.

FAMILY VACATIONS

WITH OUR FOUR CHILDREN, their spouses, and eleven grandchildren, ranging in age from five to twenty-nine, and with some of them married or with long-standing and apparently permanent partners, Rosalynn and I have had to acknowledge and respect the varied interests, obligations, and idiosyncrasies of more than two dozen people, most of whom share common genes.

In addition to our immediate kinfolks, Mary Prince is an integral member of our family. She was a young prisoner assigned to the governor's mansion when we moved there in January 1971, being punished for a crime she had not committed. Our daughter was three years old at the time, and Mary's intelligence and dedication convinced us to let her help Rosalynn care for Amy while I was governor. Designated a trusty under my care as her probation officer, she also lived with us in the White House. During this time her trial was investigated by the original sentencing judge, and it was proven that she had been framed.

It has been a difficult but enjoyable challenge for us to devise ways to share at least a portion of our lives with the other members of our immediate family. For as many years as possible our older children came home to be with us on holidays and at other special times, but once married, they had dual obligations to visit in-laws. One binding force among us is Mary Prince, who is always willing to travel to any other home when one of our children has a special need or crisis. Another tie is that we own the farmlands jointly, and we invite the children to come to Plains whenever it's convenient to ride and walk with us in the fields and woodlands, to be reminded of boundary lines and our family's history of ownership.

But as our family became more widely scattered and diverse in age, it was obvious that the older and younger ones did not know each other well and had no way to report on their year's experiences or discuss business and financial issues in which we have a common interest.

Rosalynn and I had a welcome vacation just a week after we left the White House. We were in low spirits, and I was physically exhausted after the busy lame duck congressional sessions and having stayed awake for almost three days negotiating the final release of our hostages who had been held in Iran. After I made a quick trip to Wiesbaden, Germany, to welcome all of them back to freedom and safety, we left immediately for ten days in the national park on the island of St. John, in the Virgin Islands. We swam, fished, hiked, slept, read, went sailing in large boats, and learned to windsurf. I'll always remember when Rosalynn was finally able to stay erect but didn't know how to change course and was afraid of sharks if she jumped off the surfboard far from shore. We eventually found a motorboat and caught her before she disappeared into the open sea.

In retrospect, this was our most-needed and curative vacation, and it was to be our last one for almost two years, until Royal Caribbean invited Rosalynn and me to enjoy a cruise and also receive a fee if I would give two lectures to their other passengers. After some friendly trading, we exchanged the fee for additional accommodations and weren't surprised when we had perfect family attendance. With hundreds of other vacationing families on the same ship, we were concerned that we would have little privacy, but the captain resolved the problem by issuing a personal request that we be permitted to enjoy ourselves, plus a promise that I would autograph my latest book on our last day at sea. Not only did we have plenty of time alone but I sold almost a thousand books.

It was obvious that a very attractive incentive could elevate our getting together to a top priority but that such opportunities would come rarely. We determined that by accumulating frequent flyer miles from our travels for The Carter Center, we would be able to pay the vacation expenses for everyone at least once a year, and we began ongoing discussions to develop a consensus on the most attractive destinations. Whenever their suggestions are at all rational, we try to give top priority to requests from the grandchildren.

We returned to the Virgin Islands, then enjoyed another Caribbean excursion when Rosalynn became godmother of the *Sovereign of the Seas*, at that time the largest and most elaborate cruise ship. After she smashed a huge bottle of champagne on the bow, our entire family enjoyed the cruise line's hospitality on the maiden voyage. Over the years we have taken three other cruises in the Caribbean, and they have proven to be popular with all of us.

• • •

AFTER WE OVERCAME the timidity of old age on a ski trip to Taos, this initiated at least one or two ski trips each year, usually to Crested Butte or Aspen, in addition to our regularly scheduled family outings.

On other family vacations we have visited a remote jungle resort in Belize and then an island on the barrier reef, Disney World several times, a lovely island off the Pacific coast of Panama, Oaxaca and the Yucatán Peninsula of Mexico, and the Dominican Republic.

The eruption of Popocatépetl was big news when we were in Oaxaca, so on the flight back to Mexico City I asked the pilot of Mexico's "Air Force One" to fly close enough for us to see it. We were both thrilled and frightened when he took too seriously a president's wish and our wingtip passed within a hundred yards of the smoking and spewing funnel.

We had long planned to go to Costa Rica to welcome in the new millennium, but with the frenzy about computers not being programmed to change the date properly, there were predictions of elevators failing to run, security systems being disabled, intercontinental missiles being fired inadvertently, and trains and airplanes coming to a stop, even in transit. Many people decided to go to Third World countries to avoid catastrophes, and the hotels in San José and other cities were overwhelmed with reservations. At the last minute the hotel we had chosen demanded a forty-thousand-dollar down payment, so we arranged to visit a delightful family that operated a large plantation about seventy-five miles from the capital. We enjoyed horseback riding, exploring the rain forests, and learning about the farming and ranching operation. Their custom was to have a quiet New Year's celebration at home, but we decided to welcome this especially historic event in a somewhat shady nightclub nearby.

That night someone gave me some spectacles that flashed on and off with different colors while my eyes looked out through the two middle numbers of the year 2000. With a conical hat and a big plastic nose, I thought I could be adequately disguised in case of a publicized police raid. All of us joined in the festivities, and the local celebrants prevailed on different members of our family to lead the conga lines and give dance and singing exhibitions. I mentioned to one of our new friends at midnight that at Disney World we always enjoyed a great fireworks display. He replied, "That's nothing! Come with me." He motioned for us to follow him out the back door and pointed to a nearby volcano that was erupting brilliantly into the midnight sky. Our family stood there for a long time, counting our blessings and recalling other celebrations that were not so dramatic.

AMY WAS MARRIED in 1996, and one of her wedding presents was her right to select our vacation destination for the next winter. She chose the Florida Keys, and we rented two large cottages on Summerland Key and traveled each day to different islands for fishing, swimming with dolphins, and sightseeing. We spent much of our time in Key West, with the adults having a special interest in the legacies of Harry Truman and Ernest Hemingway. Our best times were helping the smaller kids fish and catch a few crabs off the dock behind our cottage and spending long hours just sitting around and talking.

It is especially gratifying to us when our grandchildren are pleased. At the Nobel awards ceremony in Oslo in 2002, some of the world's foremost performers came to entertain, and afterward our family had a chance to meet them. The most excited one was Jeremy, now a teenager, who had several photographs taken with Michelle Branch, a beautiful young singer whom he had long admired. Later he confided to me, "The only thing that could possibly be better before I die would be to meet Shakira."

We spent our family vacation that winter in the Dominican Republic, where we had an unstructured lunch with President Hipólito Mejía's large family. After we arrived, he took me aside and said, "Mr. President, I hope you don't mind that I have invited just a few other guests." I assured him that our family would be at home with almost anyone and we would be glad to meet some of his friends. In a few minutes, the exotic young dancer-singer Shakira arrived! Jeremy's final life's dream was realized, and our family cheered when she gave him a kiss.

These annual vacations have added a new cohesion among our family members, both during the few days we are actually together in interesting and enjoyable places and throughout the year as we review past experiences and make plans for the next outing. Rosalynn and I have become better parents and grandparents as we've learned more about the interests, peculiarities, and sometimes the partially concealed problems and needs of the other two generations in our family.

I asked everyone for their comments for this book, and the overwhelming responses were about not the exotic places we've visited but the quiet times we've spent together. A frequent and most amusing memory were the various times the different generations have danced with each other. One typical e-mail message said, "The Christmas trips are the best thing you do for us. If we didn't have them, I would hardly know the other members of my family."

NOT ALL OF OUR FAMILY GATHERINGS have to be in distant places. A friend and cousin of ours located an isolated twenty-acre tract of land alongside a stream in the North Georgia mountains, and we were able to join as partners in acquiring the rustic property when we came home from the White House. We soon agreed on a site for a small log cabin, and by the time it was completed I had designed and built five beds, two armoires, eight chairs, and the tables, stools, benches, a front porch swing, and other items with which to furnish it.

Since three of our children also live in Georgia, the mountain cabin has proven to be a wonderful retreat, either for family reunions or for each of us if we desire a few days of privacy. The stream already had a population of native rainbow trout, and Georgia's Natural Resources Department also stocks it and other streams in North Georgia.

Our mountain cabin is my preferred place to write, and I often save the most difficult parts of a text or a book's closing chapter for completion there. I have a table in the loft room in front of a large picture window from which I can see and hear a waterfall that tumbles about thirty feet over stone ledges. There is a pool at the bottom that is a good place for holding trout, and one of my distractions is when there is a hatch of mayflies and the trout rise to feed on them. Dry places on the ledges are perfect for family picnics, and the trout pool is also good for a cold and refreshing swim. During proper seasons, the surroundings are colored with the blossoms of rhododendron, wild honeysuckle, and mountain laurel, or with the beautiful autumn leaves of maple, gum, oak, hickory, and sourwood. During the fall, the surface of the water is almost covered with multicolored leaves that twirl and dance in the swift currents.

Separately or together, our family can enjoy the quiet and restful good times here.

WE'VE RELISHED THE PRIVATE excursions with just our immediate family, but there are times, especially in the South, when larger gatherings are the custom. Although three branches of Rosalynn's family, the Smiths, Murrays, and Wises, have enjoyed regular reunions for several generations, my parents' relatives never had either the interest or perhaps the courage to congregate all the Gordys or Carters in the same place at the same time. While I was in the White House, Mormon leaders brought me a genealogical record of my ancestors in America back to the early 1600s. It was in orderly file folders and summarized in a leather-bound book, but I never paid it much attention until after we returned to Plains. Someone sent me "Family Tree Maker" computer software, and I entered the data in the program.

Later, one of my cousins and I decided to have a reunion of the direct descendants of our great-great-grandfather Wiley Carter, who was born in 1798 and moved from Northeast

Georgia to the Plains area after Indians were expelled in the 1830s. We set the date during his two hundredth anniversary year, but not having many current addresses, we issued a brief news bulletin that brought a deluge of responses. My computer records showed that most of them were not Wiley's descendants or even related to us, and we sent them polite notes of regret. The most delightful development was that many of our unknown relatives were located, including the entire family of Wiley's twelfth child, his youngest son, Sterling, who had run away and disappeared in Texas when he was fourteen years old.

We had planned to assemble in the auditorium of Plains High School but soon realized that we would need a much larger space. We arranged to seat our relatives in twelve groups in the basketball gymnasium of nearby Georgia Southwestern State University, and representatives of each family gave personal histories—some hilarious. Sterling served as a sheriff in Texas and came back to Georgia to woo and marry his wife, Mary. After she died in Texas, he returned to Georgia, married her sister, Loua, and returned to Texas. In his will, he directed that he "be buried between the two, but be tilted a little toward Loua."

Almost nine hundred relatives were present at this reunion, and after two days of excited reminiscences, we assembled on a hillside and had a panoramic photograph made. Since then, I've entered in my computer file all the genealogical corrections and additions that are sent to me, and I share them with one of my newfound cousins, who happens to be a Mormon with access to that church's genealogical records. Perhaps some of our great-grandchildren will repeat the process in the year 2098, in the stadium of the Atlanta Braves.

VOLUNTEER WORK

OUR WORK AT THE CARTER CENTER has provided more opportunities for binding our family and friends together in challenges, adventures, gratification, and pleasure. When we returned home to Plains in January 1981, we had no idea what we would do with the rest of our lives. We were deeply in debt, out of politics forever, unwilling to go back into the world of business and commerce, and living in a remote hamlet with no prospect of gainful employment. At fifty-six, I was one of the youngest presidents to leave the White House, and I realized that my life expectancy was at least twenty-five more years. We had to decide what to do with this time.

There was a *New Yorker* cartoon of a little boy looking up at his father and saying, "Daddy, when I grow up I want to be a former president." It was obvious that our opportunities for a full and enjoyable life were almost limitless.

After months of anguished conversations and prayers, Rosalynn and I decided to accept offers as college professors and to establish The Carter Center, patterned after Camp David, where antagonistic leaders could utilize our services as mediators. We still fulfill this role whenever opportunities arise and constantly monitor world conflicts. There are about 120 such conflicts on our current list, about 70 of which erupt into violence each year. We consider around 30 of them to be major wars—in which at least a thousand soldiers have died in combat. (In modern wars, nine civilians perish for each soldier killed.) We study every facet of these conflicts and attempt to resolve them directly or through surrogates.

Rosalynn is usually at my side when I am mediating, taking detailed notes, writing down every sentence on which there is agreement, and joining in the discussion or passing me written suggestions. Between negotiation sessions, we assess our progress and make plans for the next steps. This was an opportunity for sharing that we never had before.

Over the years, demands on The Carter Center have expanded far beyond our original concept, and each year we now monitor four or five of the most troubled elections in the world. These usually occur when a totalitarian regime is ready, for the first time, to have a democratic election or when an established democracy has an unanticipated challenge to its continued existence. When invited by the ruling party, major opposition groups, and the central election commission, we help to assure that the constitution and laws are conducive to a fair, transparent, and safe election, and send in advance teams to become familiar with the process and acquainted with the political leaders. As time for the election approaches, Rosalynn, I, and a group of volunteers are deployed to observe the actual voting procedure. After satisfactory results are attained, it is quite often necessary for us to help assure that the victors and losers accept the results with grace.

We have now gone through this procedure about fifty times in all parts of the world. Whenever it is appropriate, we invite our children to participate in an election. Perhaps the most interesting was in January 1996, when the Palestinians invited The Carter Center to monitor their choosing a president and members of a new national assembly. As members of a team of fifty observers, Amy was assigned to Bethlehem and our grandson Jason to Gaza City. The process went smoothly and successfully, with no violence.

Jeffrey is our acknowledged expert on Indonesia, and he and his wife, Annette, participated in the first democratic election ever held in this fourth largest of all nations. With forty-eight competing parties and voting on six thousand islands, this was a very complex project, but it went extremely well. We repeated the process in Indonesia five years later. Chip and Jason helped in Liberia, in an election that brought an end to a bloody war, and stayed for several weeks in an attempt to stabilize a still-troubled political situation.

Our primary effort is to help evolve a successful election, but we have had to condemn a few as fraudulent, either before votes are cast or after a false count is put forward by a dominant ruling party. On some occasions we have had to leave hurriedly for our own safety, but an overwhelming portion of our efforts have been both safe and successful.

Contrary to our original expectations, the major commitment of our Center has developed into improving the health of people who live in the poorest, most isolated and needy communities in the world. Each year we treat more than 10 million people to prevent, cure, or eradicate trachoma, river blindness, guinea worm, schistosomiasis, and elephantiasis—terrible diseases that are relatively unknown in rich nations. This work puts us in the homes of people who are suffering from these afflictions but who respond eagerly and effectively when given a chance to help themselves. In addition, we assist small farmers in Africa (who usually cultivate about two acres of land) to double or triple their production of staple food grains. We consider this to be a health project because it provides additional nutrition for many people who are extremely malnourished.

Our entire family tries to help with our work. Jack and his wife, Elizabeth, are investment bankers and are constantly searching for wealthy clients who may become contributors to our Center. In addition to his work in Liberia, Chip has played a key role in Southern Sudan during a ceasefire that we negotiated in order to promote our health programs. Jeff works regularly with our corps of student interns, teaching them about the overall concept of our work but still concentrating his research on Indonesia and other Eastern countries.

Rosalynn is a full partner in all these projects and, in addition, has become the world's foremost champion of mental health. She works to remove the stigma of mental illness in our own country and, in addition, has formed a committee of queens, first ladies, and other women leaders to pursue the same goal among their own people.

We are always eager to form partnerships with other organizations that share our goals, and we have accumulated more than 250,000 individuals who contribute regularly to help fi-

nance our work. We bring a few hundred of these key supporters to the Center in Atlanta each year for a day of briefings on
our projects, and most of them come to spend another day with
us in our hometown. Each February a similar number join us at
a ski resort in the Rocky Mountains for four days of skiing, discussions, and other enjoyable activities. It is at this event that we
have an auction, to which I always contribute an original piece
of furniture or one of my oil paintings.

It may be that some of the third world activities do not qualify as "good times" for our family and friends, but even the most
difficult and unpleasant projects are exciting and gratifying, and
they have certainly expanded our knowledge of the world and
given us a much deeper understanding of other people. It is during our many visits to these nations that we have been able to add
some of the more enjoyable experiences mentioned in this book.

SINCE LEAVING THE WHITE HOUSE and being deprived of
Air Force One, I have maintained a custom of shaking hands
with all the other passengers on each commercial plane on
which I travel before the flight takes off. It is surprising how
many old acquaintances I meet, and this custom lets me spend
the rest of the flight without a constant stream of visitors. Most
of the compliments I receive are about Rosalynn and me building houses for Habitat for Humanity.

It is true that we do this for one week each year, though it is
somewhat disconcerting to realize how little the public knows
about our work at The Carter Center for the other fifty-one
weeks. Our participation in Habitat has been quite valuable to

the organization, and we continue to enjoy serving as volunteers. Several million fund-raising letters are sent out each year over our signatures, and for more than twenty years we have led an annual "Jimmy Carter Work Project," where we are joined by a large number of other volunteers working side by side with poor families to build their new homes.

About half the time we go to a community in the United States, and these projects have included New York City, Philadelphia, Atlanta, Chicago, Miami, Houston, San Diego, Los Angeles, Milwaukee, an Indian reservation in South Dakota, and smaller communities in Appalachia, Alabama, and Georgia. We've also been to Mexico, Canada, Finland, South Korea, South Africa, and the Philippines. Our smallest project was to build ten homes in Hungary, where the word "volunteer" had a negative connotation. Under Soviet domination, the people had labored almost six days a week for wages and were then required to volunteer for additional hours of work. Our entire workforce came to the village of Vác from other countries, but after Rosalynn and I became friends with some fishermen on the nearby Danube River and explained what we were doing, they poured in to help us during the last few days.

When our annual project moved to South Korea in 2001, we were unable to obtain approval from Pyongyang to build houses in North Korea, but they had no objection to our doing so in the Demilitarized Zone. We were amused a few months later when President George W. Bush announced that he would be visiting "the most dangerous place in the world" and realized that it was in the neutralized area between the two Koreas—where we had recently helped to complete eight homes.

Our largest project has been in the Philippines, where thirteen thousand volunteers helped us complete 293 homes—all constructed, as usual, in just five days. These were tiny homes by American standards, just three hundred square feet, but the new homeowners were deeply grateful. I remember most vividly the woman who had been living with five children inside an abandoned septic tank.

Some volunteers have joined us for fifteen or twenty years, and for them the annual events are a great reunion. Obviously, this work also involves us intimately with the local community. At the completion of the week's work, we give each family a Bible and the key to their house, and I usually make a brief dedication speech. Sometimes there is a serious language barrier, and we had a special treat in South Africa. With each group I would introduce our grandson Jason to say a few words, and the somnolent audience, not having understood what I was saying, would first be surprised, then become alert and applaud vigorously when he translated my talk into fluent Zulu, which he had learned while in the Peace Corps.

I believe that almost every human being has a desire to know and perhaps to serve other people, including those in a completely different social and economic realm of life. Despite good intentions, it is very difficult to cross such a chasm, and The Carter Center and Habitat have provided us with this opportunity. Our projects in many nations often have been severely challenging, but any difficulties have been far exceeded by the glow of pride and gratitude on the faces of people who, for the first time in their lives, will be free of disease, own a decent home, or have a chance to live in peace and choose their own leaders.

CLIMBING TOWARD EVEREST

OSALYNN AND I DECIDED to try something different in 1984: climbing to the base camp below Mount
Everest in Nepal. In addition to our normal jogging,
biking, and tennis, we lifted weights to prepare for carrying
backpacks along the steep trails. We wanted no rain and minimal
snow at the higher altitudes and chose mid-October as the best
time for good weather. When we arrived in Kathmandu and prepared for our first foray to the high mountains, however, the entire subcontinent was enduring an unseasonal monsoon, and the
city was drenched.

We had first planned to go westward, ascending from the
capital's 4,500 feet to more than twice that altitude in the Annapurna region. Then, more acclimated to the thin air, we would
helicopter over to Namche Bazar, a village on the way to Mount
Everest at an altitude of 11,300 feet, remain there a day or two,
and begin climbing past some ancient Buddhist monasteries
to Pheriche, at 14,000 feet. Having just passed my sixtieth birthday, I would probably not want to climb any higher than this.

With the persistent rain and fog, our original plans had to be abandoned. Our hotel radio reported that a team of thirty-two New Zealanders were stranded in the unexpected deep snow in the Annapurna region, and four of them had been lost in an avalanche. Several other groups were reporting severe difficulty at the higher altitudes because of the weather. We did fly westward in a dense fog but returned after spending one night on the way to Annapurna. Since it had been raining for seven days and there was no break in sight, we decided to skip Annapurna and finally managed to be airlifted directly to Namche Bazar in one of the helicopters heading higher for possible rescue operations.

Our guide, Pasang Kami Sherpa, met us at the Shyangboche airstrip and said, "Just call me P.K. Your helicopter ride saved you seventeen days of walking, but we'll be on the ground from now on." When we arrived at his lodge in Namche Bazar, there was a sign on the door: CLOSED THREE DAYS. PRESIDENT CARTER VISIT. We found the village beautiful, filled with clear evidence of the villagers' Buddhist faith, and the shops crammed with the most luxurious foods and mountain-climbing supplies. These were surpluses left by climbing parties after they descended from Everest.

Our bed was a wooden platform on which we slept in sleeping bags, fully clothed except for our shoes. It was still damp and cold. After all this time, we had not been able to see a mountain through the thick clouds and fog.

The next morning we peeked out of our window and had a breathtaking view of Thamserku peak, 22,000 feet high and entirely covered with the new-fallen snow. Since we had just made a 7,000-foot increase in altitude, P.K. recommended that we remain for a day or so at about this level. We decided to make an overnight visit to Thame, a strenuous five-hour hike along the Bhote Kosi River. Rosalynn said it was the worst day of the entire trip but still a pleasant change from the inside of a hotel room to the outside beauty of the Himalayas. This was a heavily traveled route into Tibet, and we met a number of people carrying heavy loads of potatoes and other produce for sale in Namche. We were always greeted with hands together as in prayer, a nod, and the word "Namaste." There were frequent deposits of prayer stones or large carved rocks in the middle of the trail, and we learned quickly to pass on the left side, so that going to and fro would result in a clockwise circumambulation.

Completely exhausted after the day's trek along the steep side of the ravine, we collapsed in our sleeping bags at Thame, but P.K. was soon there saying that supper was ready and suggesting that we hike even higher to see the ancient monastery. All of us were hoping that Rosalynn would decline and give us a chance to stay in camp, but she agreed, and we made the hike. We saw two remarkable birds: blood pheasants and the rare Nepalese national bird, which P.K. called "damphes." They have feathers of nine colors, with a blue topknot.

After a night in our tents, we returned to Namche Bazar, retracing our steps high above the river. While en route we witnessed a remarkable scene. A landslide had resulted from the steady rain, and roots were exposed from a forest that had been harvested long ago for firewood. Women and children were on the slope digging furiously to obtain armloads of roots, while chunks of earth and stone still whizzed by their heads. Now we understood more clearly why army troops had to be stationed among the few remaining trees in the area to prevent a complete devastation of the woodlands.

After a night's sleep at P.K.'s lodge, we began our trek toward the world's highest peak, with a total of twelve in our climbing party, including some Secret Service agents especially chosen for their physical prowess. We were amazed to learn that there were fifteen yaks, forty porters, and twenty male and female Sherpas required to carry our tents, food, and other supplies. The total cost to each of us was just forty dollars a day! The almost constant rain had now turned to intermittent snow, and the trails were slick whenever the temperature rose above freezing.

We soon met a group of Japanese climbers who had been turned back at the Everest base camp because of the weather. I asked them how deep the snow had been, and one of them put his hand just below his chin. When I asked for their advice for us, there was a half-joking chorus, "Turn back! Turn back!" Despite this, we decided to press on.

At the end of the day, we had been up and down steep slopes on both sides of a river, with a final climb of about 2,500 feet to Tengboche monastery. A music and dance service was held in honor of the young spiritual leader (rinpoche), and I noticed that he followed the ceremony by reading along in an ornate manuscript with gold lettering, obviously valuable and ancient. I asked him who wrote the script, and he replied, "I did." Believing that he had misunderstood me, I started to repeat my question, but P.K. leaned over and whispered, "He did it in one of his previous lives."

We were high in the snow-covered mountains now, and Rosalynn and I put our sleeping bags together, covered ourselves with a heavy yak-wool blanket, left our clothes on, and cuddled against each other and hot water bags. We managed to get some sleep but found our drinking water flasks frozen solid inside the tent when we awoke the next morning. The climbing was more difficult that day, and we were glad to arrive at Pheriche, at 14,000 feet, where there was a medical rescue mission. It was staffed by an American nurse and doctor, two women who had volunteered to serve here during the three-month trekking season. Clothed always in ski outfits to keep warm, they were hospitable but especially glad to see us because our presence permitted them to make a fire in a tiny stove in their hut. They exclaimed, "Only a president could bring us a privilege so rare!"

We stayed two days at this rest stop, during which time three of the men had to be evacuated by helicopter to the hospital in Kathmandu because of altitude sickness. One was a regular competitor in the Hawaii triathlon, and another ran marathons in less than two hours and twenty minutes. There is no way to predict who will succumb to this potentially fatal affliction that rapidly fills either the brain or lungs with fluids.

Estimating the distance we still had to cover to reach the base camp, we set a faster pace when we began climbing again. Twenty paces from our lunch stop at 15,200 feet, Rosalynn developed a severe headache and had to lie down for a few minutes to control nausea. When she recovered enough to sit up, we had a difficult argument with her, and she finally agreed to return to Pheriche, where the doctor could give her a good examination. Watching her walk sturdily down the trail, I was confident that she would fully recover.

We had now lost more than half our original party, and two others were stopping every now and then to throw up. I decided to continue, but it wasn't the same without Rosalynn, and even P.K. was concerned about the groaning and slight movements of the high walls of ice and snow that bordered our path. We spent that night at Lobuje, just above 16,000 feet, and were thankful that our guide produced a small can of charcoal with which we could partially dry our soaked stockings. After consulting maps of the area, I set an ambitious goal of reaching a peak called Kala Pattar (black pinnacle) about 1,100 feet above the base camp and with a superb view of Mount Everest. This would require a strenuous effort for six hours, then a fairly rapid return descent to Pheriche before dark.

We had breakfast at 4:30 A.M. and were on the narrow, frozen trail a half hour later, stumbling along with flashlights and trying to minimize the number of times we fell. The weather was perfectly clear, the most beautiful night sky I had ever seen. Daylight revealed Mount Everest in all its grandeur, looming above us. My personal guide, Ang Tsering, and I had moved several hundred yards ahead of our companions, and as we reached a place called Gorak Shep (black crow), he touched my arm and pointed ahead. There were nine Himalayan snow cocks sitting on a ledge, and we watched as they swooped over our heads and sailed down toward the base camp. We could also see that all the other members of our party were returning to Lobuje.

I was almost exhausted, but after a brief rest I resolved to climb on up to Kala Pattar. It was a much more precipitous path than any we had seen, and the rocks were all covered with a layer of ice. We finally neared the top and were surprised to see two men there, with a telescope focused on the south col of Mount Everest. They were even more astonished when they recognized me. I soon learned that they were part of an expedition from India, which was having a tragic experience on Everest. Five of the party had already perished when their tent blew off the mountain, and with a radio and a telescope these two men were consulting with the remaining climbers on their next move. I was asked to talk to them on the radio, and I expressed my admiration for their courage and my personal condolences on their loss. They informed me that they would continue their climb, since the weather had greatly improved.

We were far behind schedule but decided to descend by a circuitous route that was much safer. It was after 9:00 P.M. when we arrived at Pheriche and learned that Rosalynn was feeling fine and had flown back to Kathmandu. I declined supper, crawled into my sleeping bag under the heavy blanket, and slept soundly. The next morning I found that my hands were bleeding, my fingernails split, both shins were skinned, and I had bruises on my legs and buttocks. Despite these vivid reminders of a difficult climb, I was thankful for one of my life's most exciting and gratifying experiences. We flew back to Namche Bazar in just eight minutes, over steep and winding trails that had required three full days on foot.

Twenty-four hours later, Rosalynn and I were in a howdah on the back of a huge elephant, wading across streams and through high grass to the Royal Chitwan National Park. This was on the Indian border, and we were immersed in a lowland environment of Bengal tigers, rhinos, enormous crocodiles, pythons, and cobras. We were a long way from Plains, Georgia!

KILIMANJARO

ONE OF THE MAJOR PROJECTS we launched the year after going to Nepal was to teach African farmers how to grow more food grain for their family use, with any surplus available to be sold. Their family farms are tiny by American standards—only one hectare, or two acres each. With the project to be financed by a Japanese foundation, we decided to go into twelve African nations, eventually involving about 600,000 farmers. In order to spread out the seasons, the first phase would be in two countries north of the equator and two in the south. One of them was Tanzania, and we soon had 50,000 farmers learning how to double or triple their production of maize. When I went to visit some of these farmers in 1987, President Ali Hassan Mwinyi accompanied me to an area near the base of Mount Kilimanjaro, and while there he extended an invitation to bring some of our family to explore the game parks and consider a climb of the highest peak in Africa. The Everest experience had been so exciting, challenging, and in the end enjoyable—at least to me—that I was eager to accept.

When I mentioned his invitation that winter, there was a burst of enthusiasm from our family, and we began to seek a time when some of the younger Carters could make the trip. Finally, all the arrangements were made, and we set aside nine days in early August. Traveling with Rosalynn and me were our son Jack and his wife, Judy, Chip, and our three oldest grandchildren, Jason (age thirteen), James (eleven), and Sarah Rosemary (nine). We were warned that only one trekker in eight is expected to reach the top but assured that even a partial climb would be a delightful experience. The standard cost for the five-day excursion was about the same as one night in a big-city hotel.

After a twenty-four-hour trip across eight time zones, we spent our first night in the Kibo Hotel near the base of the mountain and the next morning drove to the park entrance, at an altitude of 6,000 feet. Our chief guide was Major General Mirisho Sarakikya, who said he had climbed Mount Kilimanjaro twenty-seven times. He issued each of us a steel-tipped walking staff, which Rosalynn rejected until the general explained that at higher altitudes she would be unable to sit down, rest, and then rise again without it. He taught us a few Swahili phrases, emphasizing that the most important was *poli poli,* which means "very slowly." Chip taught everyone else a chant: "Go fast and you won't last. Go slow and you'll see snow."

Kilimanjaro has a classic volcano shape, with gentle slopes at the base and increasing steepness as the cone is approached. The first day we climbed for five hours on a trail through a rain forest, which was very slick, forcing us to grasp exposed tree roots to support ourselves. The frequent afternoon showers sent streams of mud and water down the narrow path and around our feet, often over the tops of our boots. Almost everyone was in good spirits and still excited about the adventure: Rosalynn enjoyed the brilliant flowers, James and Sarah competed to see who could sight more blue monkeys, and Chip said it was just like a Tarzan movie. But Jason said, several times, "I'm not having a very good time." After arriving at Mandara Camp (9,000 feet), he and Judy expressed a desire to wait there for the rest of us to return, but we wanted to keep the family together and finally persuaded them to proceed for another day.

Since the trail was predicted to be dry, we changed from wet boots to running shoes, and the walking was much easier. At about 10,000 feet we broke out of the forest and finally had our first clear view of the snow-covered peak. It seemed that our wide trail was going through a set from *The Sound of Music,* and our guides taught us how to recognize the various gentians, buttercups, wild iris, gladiolus, heather, and a species of protea. About halfway through our day's journey, we began to see giant lobelias, as high as nine feet, a few of them blossoming. There was a permeating scent of sage.

With wide visibility, someone counted thirty-five members of our party, including some representatives of the government, our guides, porters, and a few Tanzanian news reporters. There were additional luggage carriers, who left long before we did each morning in order to set up camps where we would stop for a noonday rest and later spend the nights. (I learned later that the general had strict orders from President Mwinyi to be sure that I made it to the top, even if other members of our family had to turn back at a lower altitude.)

After trekking steadily upward for eleven miles in seven hours, we arrived at Horombo Camp, about 12,500 feet above sea level and surrounded by a sparse growth of even larger and stranger trees called senecios. As on other days, we reached our destination at midafternoon, had a long nap, then awoke for supper. Many of us had lost our appetites, but knowing that we should maintain our strength, we tried to swallow as much of the soup, boiled vegetables, and bread as possible. Then we would sleep for about eleven hours, trying to stay warm and go out into the frigid night to urinate as few times as possible.

Horombo was as high as Judy wanted to go, and we realized later that all of us should have paused here for at least a day of rest and acclimatization to the higher altitude. We decided to celebrate Jason's birthday while his mother was still with us, so before moving on the next day we inflated a plastic cake with thirteen artificial candles on top. Despite the special occasion, our entire group was uncharacteristically subdued, and General Sarakikya tried to rejuvenate our spirits. He congratulated us on achieving this height and said that Sir Edmund Hillary, after having climbed Mount Everest, had to turn back before reaching the crater of Mount Kilimanjaro. He also commented, with more descriptive words, that it was natural for some of us, even our experienced porters, to "throw out" on occasion.

We stopped every hour or so to eat a snack and drink as much water and tea as possible to avoid dehydration in the thin air and direct sunlight. We learned the value of the walking sticks as we struggled to stand after sitting down to rest on a boulder or outcropping of rock. Some of our group refused to sit down at all, convinced that they could never rise again.

The first five groups we met had failed to reach the summit, although one had made it to Hans Meyer cave, about halfway between Kibo and the top. This was discouraging, but then we met two experienced Japanese climbers who said they had looked into the crater. As we approached the rest camp, Rosalynn said, "All my muscles hurt, my knees are weak, my nose is bleeding, and my head aches, but I'm still feeling much better now than I did this morning." We had trekked for ten miles up 3,300 feet and were now at the same elevation as the top of Mont Blanc, the highest mountain in the European Alps.

Without any prior notice, General Sarakikya notified us at suppertime that we would be divided into three groups for our final ascent, to begin shortly after midnight. I would be in the first group, Jack and Chip in the next, and Rosalynn and the children in the third. He said he had been observing our performance during the past few days and wanted to give everyone the best opportunity to succeed. I was exhausted and realized only later that I should have objected, because he was practicing triage—dividing us according to our chances of reaching the crater.

It was already snowing when we began climbing the next morning, and we found that the trail was very steep, so that we had to make wide zigzags across what the guides called "scree." This was completely loose fragments of flat stone that slid downward with every step. We stopped for ten minutes to rest at Hans Meyer cave, then resumed climbing. For the first time the guides were urging us to increase our pace. Both we and our porters were stopping frequently to rest and "throw out." Seeing Jack's group struggling to catch up, I forced our leaders to stop and wait for our two sons.

I became confused and aggravated after we asked the guides about the distance to the top. The first answer was "only 200 more meters." Having competed in the 100-meter dash as a student, I was relieved to hear this good news, but after fifteen minutes of hard climbing the answer was "150 meters more." It took me a while to realize that we were discussing altitude and not distance, but for the last half hour the two were almost the same because the trail was so steep. Most of our companions dropped behind, but Jack, Chip, and I reached the top just at sunrise, in a blinding snowstorm. As we stood there, proud but somewhat disappointed by the limited view, a gust of strong wind increased visibility enough for us to see across the crater. We signed the book and entered the unforgettable date: 8-8-88.

I learned later that Rosalynn had started out with the three grandchildren but that they hadn't gone a hundred yards before demanding to return to camp. By the time she was climbing again, she was at least two hours behind our lead group, and it took her four hours to reach the cave, at 17,000 feet. After resting for a while, she climbed another half hour and finally decided to turn back. I've always believed that, with me, she could have made it to the summit.

We began to descend and decided to conduct an experiment as soon as the weather cleared somewhat. My sons and I had been avid Frisbee throwers since our days in Georgia's governor's mansion, when all our children were with us. We had devised an "eighteen-hole" course around the mansion grounds, with trees, bushes, ditches, fences, buildings, and flower beds serving as either handicaps or final targets. I remember that when Delta Air Lines made its inaugural flight to Mexico City, they invited me to go, and I asked my sons to serve as my surrogates. At the airport the boys threw their Frisbees back and forth and, unfortunately for Delta, almost all the news coverage was about their skills in this activity. Rosalynn and I had thrown Frisbees at high altitudes both in Nepal and in Tibet, and I decided to throw one of the discs as far as possible from a relatively level spot near the top of Kilimanjaro. After being launched, it sailed straight down the mountain, swerved far to the right, then back left, and all of us cheered as it landed only ten feet from the trail.

Our descent was perhaps even more dangerous, with the slick and icy mud, loose rocks, and our increased speed. We arrived back at Kibo at eight-thirty, only a few minutes after Rosalynn. I hugged her and said, "Rosalynn, I think I've climbed my last mountain." She replied, "Thank God!" We slept a few hours and then began a surprisingly enjoyable trip to the lowest camp, hiking eighteen miles the last day. We had a congratulatory message from President Mwinyi and a request that we come to Dar es Salaam to receive our official certificates. Regardless of the ultimate height climbed, everyone in the family had a great sense of pleasure and achievement. Although we had not changed clothes or bathed in five days and had walked or climbed for sixty miles, we were soon making plans for a return to Kilimanjaro or to explore another peak.

WE STOPPED IN KENYA on the way home, and after a shopping excursion we had difficulty in finding room in our loaned corporate jet for carved animals, especially some large wooden giraffes. Our next stop was Cairo, Egypt, where we visited the pyramids and some of the nearby antiquities. Early on our last morning, I took the family to a camel auction, where hundreds were on sale, both those for riding and others to be slaughtered for food. When the chief auctioneer learned that we were there, he insisted on giving us one of his most beautiful young camels, which he said had just arrived from Northern Sudan. "You will find the meat delicious, and very tender," he said. Our youngest granddaughter, Sarah Rosemary, astonished him by replying, "We don't have room for a camel. Our plane is already full of giraffes!"

The donor refused to keep the camel, insisting that it already belonged to our family and he couldn't accept a gift from us. Finally, we arranged for the camel to be accepted by U.S. Embassy personnel and delivered to Mother Teresa's local home for orphan children. Back in Plains, we found that Walter Cronkite had learned of the incident, and several evening news broadcasts ended with the latest information about the orphans' having fallen in love with the animal and refusing to have it harmed. Eventually, they agreed that it be sold, for six hundred dollars, with a promise that it would be trained for riding.

WATCHING BIRDS TOGETHER

FTER CLIMBING MOUNT KILIMANJARO, we visited several Tanzanian game parks and hired a small van and driver. We began this excursion with a contest between us adults and the grandchildren to see who could first sight a new species of animal. After a day or so, we had run out of warthogs, wildebeests, baboons, dik-diks, mongeese, various kinds of monkeys, and the larger animals. One of our most life-changing surprises evolved when we learned that our driver was a highly trained ornithologist, who began quietly to call out the common and Latinized names of each bird we saw. Our contest quickly changed to superb starlings, sunbirds, barbets, whydahs, and weavers. Within three days we had recorded 126 species of birds.

Rosalynn and I soon realized that bird-watching was something we could do together, perhaps for the rest of our lives—either in distant nations or from our breakfast room window. This pursuit has added a new and exciting dimension to all our trips, and through it we have made a completely new circle of friends. There is a "breeder bird survey" that begins on the first Saturday in June near our home and has followed the exact same route for many years. We have accompanied the experts several times as they look and listen for precisely three minutes, move forward one-half mile, and repeat this process for about four hours. This permits their collective reports, year after year, to reveal any variations in the prevalence or absence of species as the local environment and other factors change.

One morning, after we had completed the standard tour, I was standing in our front yard with the more experienced birders. I said, "I see that you have yellow-billed cuckoos on your Georgia list, and we've heard one or two, but I've been living here all my life and never sighted one." One of the birders happened to look up and replied, "There go a pair of them flying over us."

There is excitement when a new species is sighted in our area. Last year, for the first time, we learned that there were three nesting pairs of painted buntings just nine miles from our home. This is a bird of extraordinary beauty, and all the birders in the area soon descended on the site to add another sighting to their lists. We keep a pair of binoculars and a book of bird species on our breakfast table, and the first arrivals of migrating finches or ruby-throated hummingbirds, or seasonal plumage changes, have added a new level of pleasure to our lives.

Since our Tanzania visit, we have tried as often as possible to schedule birding expeditions in the countries we visit. Well in advance we ask the hotel manager or U.S. ambassador to arrange for a trained naturalist to go with us, and we take a couple of hours in the mornings to visit a city park, a wooded farm area, or perhaps a seashore to add a few species to our lifetime list. We have not only a shelf full of bird books for different locations but also a computerized list that includes the nine thousand species known in the world. It is especially interesting to learn as much as possible about the habits and idiosyncrasies of each species we sight. Now we appreciate the birds that are around our own home and farm as much as the more exotic ones we discover for the first time.

We had always just added a few hours to an existing Carter Center business trip for bird-watching until recently, when we arranged for three full days of birding in the Lower Rio Grande Valley of Texas. This is a special area for American birders, with access to the Gulf shore, deserts, the river, and heavily wooded areas, its extreme southern location, and its position on migratory routes between North and South America. Accompanied by new birding friends, we observed a total of 151 species, 57 of them seen by us for the first time in the United States. Even the experts were excited when we observed the tropical parula, clay-colored robin, aplomado falcon (once almost extinct), and the extremely rare short-tailed hawk.

Perhaps our most interesting sighting occurred when we visited our son Jack in Bermuda. There is a species known as a Bermuda petrel (cahow) that was believed to be extinct for more than three hundred years. To everyone's surprise and delight, a local ornithologist, Dr. David Wingate, discovered some of the birds nesting on a tiny, isolated islet. He invited us to join him in a visit to the nesting site. Thinking that we were privy to some special information, we were somewhat disappointed to learn that our Texas birding friends were completely informed about the entire history of the cahow.

As is well known, the whooping crane is another species that was facing extinction until a few years ago, when only twenty of the birds survived. A remarkable program was begun to take the few available eggs and increase the total flock. The hatchlings in captivity never see their real mothers or a human being but are taught that a volunteer covered completely in a white suit and with an arm extension resembling a female adult's neck and head is their parent. When partially grown, they transfer their filial loyalty to an ultralight aircraft and learn to run alongside as it taxis on the ground. When able to fly, the young cranes follow the aircraft into the air in a wedge-shaped formation off of its wings. Eventually they take off from their birth sites in Wisconsin and fly about sixty miles each day behind the aircraft, landing each evening in a prearranged secluded place. They are penned at night to prevent straying and for protection against bobcats, foxes, and coyotes. Fortunately, their annual flight path is very near our home in Plains, and Rosalynn and I have helped the regular volunteers with this task.

The young birds overwinter in a natural refuge in Florida, then return unassisted along the same route to their northern breeding grounds. Fortunately, there are now 430 whooping cranes alive, about three-fourths of them living in the wild and about a hundred in captivity providing eggs for increasing the flocks.

Birding is exciting even in metropolitan areas. More than one hundred species of birds have been sighted in the heart of

Atlanta on the thirty-acre grounds of The Carter Center, and one of the most active groups of bird-watchers give close attention to Central Park in New York City. Some wonderful aspects of birding are that almost anyone can adopt it as a hobby, the opportunity for increasing knowledge is unlimited, and even the most disparate bird-watchers are bound together with the intensity of their common interest and the friendly competition that develops among them.

PANMUNJOM TO MOUNT FUJI

OSALYNN AND I HAVE VISITED numerous foreign nations for projects of The Carter Center, but perhaps the most interesting and significant was our attempt to prevent a possible catastrophic war on the Korean Peninsula. Under the leadership of President Kim Il Sung, North Korea had reluctantly placed supervision of its nuclear reactor program under the International Atomic Energy Agency. In 1994, however, they had removed nine thousand spent fuel rods from their old power plant and seemed to be preparing to purify this radioactive material so that it could be used for nuclear weapons. International criticism aroused their nationalistic pride, and they responded by turning off surveillance cameras and announcing that IAEA inspectors would be expelled from the country.

The U.S. government's ill-advised policy of not communicating directly with the government in Pyongyang had ended in a stalemate, with the United States seeking to impose increasingly severe economic and political sanctions from the United Nations on the small, isolated, impoverished, and mysterious

Communist nation. Kim Il Sung had sought my help as a mediator for almost three years, but he was a dictator whom I had despised since my Korean War service as a submariner, and I was naturally suspicious of his motives. He continued to send emissaries with attractive messages about his willingness to resolve the nuclear impasse; still, even when I decided to participate, I had not been able to obtain approval from the White House. In June 1994 some Chinese friends told me that the North Koreans would launch an all-out attack on South Korea if their nation were publicly condemned and their revered (even worshiped) leader branded an outlaw, and this opinion was confirmed to me by the U.S. ambassador in Seoul.

Rosalynn and I decided to go to Pyongyang and attempt to defuse the crisis without approval from Washington. We informed President Bill Clinton of our intentions, and he finally granted tacit approval for our trip. After receiving a superficial briefing in Washington that later proved to be based on incorrect intelligence, we flew to Seoul and met with South Korea's President Kim Young Sam and the American general Gary Luck, commanding officer of American and South Korean military forces. They shared my concerns and estimated that casualties from a preemptive North Korean attack would exceed those of the Korean War.

The next day we crossed the Demilitarized Zone and drove about 125 miles northward to Pyongyang, the first Americans to make this direct trip since the end of the Korean War in 1951. There were just a few trucks and no other passenger cars on the wide four-lane highway, and I asked our North Korean

escort a stream of questions about agriculture, sports, education, religion, and other aspects of life in the homes and small
villages as we passed. In answers that seemed carefully prepared,
he described an idyllic existence. I had no way to contradict
him, except that as an experienced farmer I could tell there was
little fertilizer being used, plant populations were very sparse by
our standards, and some of the furrows ran almost directly up
and down the hills instead of following contours to prevent soil
erosion.

We were received in the capital like royalty and ensconced in
luxurious guest quarters near the Taedong River. I had a complete agenda of concerns from the White House and a few special goals of my own, and was able to present them to the North
Korean officials the first afternoon. We found our interlocutors
to be quite reluctant to make any concessions or agreements,
but the situation changed completely the following morning,
when the president joined the discussions.

Kim Il Sung was surprisingly knowledgeable about the de-
tails of reactor technology and had unquestioned authority.
When he asked any of his top ministers a question, they jumped
out of their chairs, stood rigidly erect, and gave the answer
with the impeccable protocol of a military subordinate. By that
evening President Kim had agreed to all the U.S. demands
concerning the nuclear issues, and the next morning he invited
Rosalynn and me to join him and his wife on his son's pleasure
yacht for a trip of about sixty miles down the river to the sea. We
had an interesting conversation during the seven-hour journey,
and he seemed to agree with all my suggestions, including an

agreement for an unprecedented summit meeting between him and South Korean President Kim Young Sam to be arranged by me at an early date.

Kim Il Sung was an excellent guide on our trip, able to explain in detail everything of interest we could see on the banks of the river. He knew exactly when every grain silo had been erected and the harvested crop to be stored in each and was equally familiar with parks, schoolhouses, boat landings, bridges, and most of the fields. It was obvious that, as an unchallenged dictator for the past fifty years, he had been personally responsible for all the significant decisions concerning his country, and he refused to acknowledge any of the abysmal economic and social problems that we knew existed.

The president knew Rosalynn and I were avid fly-fishers and told us that when he returned from exile and prison as a liberator he had visited the northeast mountain area of his country. The peasants along the rivers were attempting to poison all the trout, calling them "Japanese fish." Kim informed them that they had been imported by American engineers early in the century, and he and they initiated a program for protection of the fish. He invited us to return when convenient to try the fishing, and to help him organize visits by other fly-fishers from the United States and Europe.

Although there were very few vehicles on the superhighway between the Demilitarized Zone and Pyongyang, and practically no private automobiles, the capital city was perfectly manicured, great beds of flowers were everywhere, and at night all the buildings were illuminated as though it was Christmas in New York. We rode on the subway, deep below the ground, and found it ornately decorated with ceramic murals. Our guides took us to a huge department store, which was filled with customers examining a wide array of consumer goods. Our impression, though, was that a lot of this was superficial ornamentation, and it may have been that—even with less than a week's notice—the North Koreans had somehow put on an elaborate show for us.

The entertainment was truly breathtaking. Hundreds of talented actors and musicians performed spectacular plays equivalent to any at Disney World or on Broadway. In one of them, there was a presentation of the history of Western music, including classical, folk, swing, country and western, jazz, and bebop. With eyes closed we could easily envision the Metropolitan Opera, and Glenn Miller, Nat King Cole, Louis Armstrong, and Elvis Presley, with their lyrics in impeccable English. We visited one of the huge training and education centers for children and found them learning skills in academic subjects, art, drama, music, foreign languages, handicrafts, and different sports. The most memorable demonstration was in the natatorium, where a line of children were waiting on the ten-meter diving platform for us to enter. With music playing, the youngsters dove one by one, teenagers doing fancy dives and the last ones seeming to be only about five years old.

Kim Il Sung soon repeated all his commitments to President Clinton, but he died just a few weeks after we left, while visiting the site of the scheduled summit meeting with South Korean leaders. Quite slowly and reluctantly, some of our agreements were implemented by his administration before President Clinton left office, but since then our government has refused to negotiate or have direct talks with the North Korean leaders, and once again there is a crisis involving the status of their nuclear development program and the possibility of our alleviating their fears about a military attack.

It may be necessary in the future for us to make another visit to North Korea—either to negotiate a peace agreement or to catch a few "American" fish!

We have visited Japan often to promote the projects of The Carter Center. After fishing on the lower slopes of Mount Fuji in 1981, we contemplated going to the top. In 1994, after our visit to North Korea, we invited Japanese friends to join us. None of them had ever made the climb, and I assured them it would not tax their capabilities, since Fuji's summit is more than a mile below the heights I had achieved in Nepal and Tanzania.

Most people stop partway up to spend the night in one of the rest camps, then climb to the peak and descend the next day. Because we had previous experience, I thought that, with an early start, we could make the round trip in one day. It had been only five months since I had torn the ligaments of my left knee skiing, but I had played tennis with my steel brace and had little pain when I walked or climbed stairs. Since the muscles were still weak, I would wear the brace just to be exceptionally careful.

Sure enough, we kept a steady, moderate pace up the increasingly steep slope, letting Rosalynn lead our line of climbers. It was a warm July day, and we soon shed our sweaters and were stopping frequently to drink water or lemonade. The last few hundred yards were quite steep, but the trail was well established, and the rough edges had been worn off by the mostly Japanese climbers who had made the ascent for centuries. We reached the peak as scheduled, rested, ate a nice lunch, and prepared to descend.

Our guide was an older gentleman (I was seventy) who had performed this duty for more than forty years, and he was proud and excited to have a former president under his care. He told us that a new route down the mountain had been recently completed, primarily for service personnel, and suggested that by using it we might have an experience that other tourists could not enjoy.

This proved a terrible mistake. The new trail was still covered with loose dirt, small round gravel, and shale, and it led almost straight down. I found every step down the steep slope—a combination of walking and sliding—very painful. I was soon sweating profusely and dropped to the end of the procession so the others would not notice that I was in trouble. I began to call out more frequently for rest stops, and Rosalynn came back to inquire about me. She suggested that we arrange for a medical team to carry me down on a litter, but I quickly rejected such an embarrassing admission of my weakness.

I struggled halfway down the mountain, until my swollen knee stretched tight against the inside of the steel brace and waves of nausea began to sweep over me. The entire group stopped at one of the switchbacks, and I saw some climbers nearby, ascending the mountain on the ancient trail. I asked our guide if we could go over to where the packed and worn path would give me firm footing, and he agreed. After that, my pain was bearable, and we completed our descent about two hours later than we had planned.

When we arrived back at our hotel, CNN International was reporting that a small storm had remained immobile over our area of Georgia, and in Plains it had rained twenty-three inches in a single day. The floodwaters had inundated more than fifteen hundred homes, many of them totally destroyed, and thirty-one people were drowned. Every highway and railroad bridge around Plains was washed away, and water was above the tops of the windows in our small farm cabin near Kinchafoonee Creek. After all, not all of our days can be good ones.

SPAIN

Whenever possible, we try to combine work with pleasure. In 1998 I had an invitation to give a lecture to an important audience in Santander, on the northern border of Spain, and Rosalynn and I decided to use this opportunity to talk about the work of The Carter Center. We would follow my speech by meandering westward through the country and then returning to Madrid, before going south to Granada and Seville. Since Annette had studied Spanish with Rosalynn while she and Jeff lived in the White House, we invited them to join us. During our brief visit, we wanted to learn as much as possible about the country and its people.

The Spanish government has established inns called *paradors,* either newly constructed or in ancient buildings, near many of the large cities and historic sites. We arranged for lodging in a different one each night, spaced so that we would cover our route of about 1,500 miles in ten days. The best thing about the trip was that we had no itinerary except to reach the night's *parador,* leaving each day free to do whatever we decided in the morning. Since we usually had lived by a strict travel schedule for many years, this freedom in itself was like a vacation.

I had lost six hours of my birthday when we changed time zones en route to Spain. Before I delivered my speech, we visited the remarkable Guggenheim art museum in Bilbao. Located alongside a river in the industrial part of the city, the huge building seems to flow outward in waves from a central axis almost two hundred feet high, providing nineteen galleries of great flexibility and diversity. One of them housed a display that told the history of Chinese art for the past five thousand years. In another, we enjoyed meeting Robert Rauschenberg, who was busy arranging a vast work of his, which he called his "one-quarter-mile" painting. It was, in fact, that long, and the gallery is large enough to accommodate it.

Bilbao is in the center of Basque country, but I was still surprised to learn how many people were aware that The Carter Center had been involved in exploring reconciliation between the Spanish government and the Basques. The most militant Basque separatist faction, ETA, had used the same tactics as the IRA in Ireland but recently had made a pledge of nonviolence, and there were at least discussions of a peace effort. At a fervent request from Spanish officials, I emphasized that the best approach was direct talks between Basques and the government, without any foreign mediation. (If needed, of course, we would be glad to help.)

As we began our vacation, we had, as Washington Irving said when he visited Spain in 1829, "a genuine disposition to be pleased." Like him, we were not to be disappointed. The highlight, never to be exceeded, was a visit to the prehistoric cave at Altamira. In order not to disturb the temperature and humidity, only twenty people, five at a time, can enter it each day. There is a waiting list of a year or more. We had seen a few photographs of the prehistoric paintings, but we were not prepared for their brilliance and beauty, the large number, and the sensitivity with which the artists had presented the bison, deer, and horses— seventeen thousand years ago! The government was creating an exact replica of the cave, which will permit many more people to have a similar experience.

In León we toured the house of Antonio Gaudi, the famous architect from Barcelona who obviously had a great time de signing the flamboyant building. He loved to do intriguing and often ridiculous things, and his style certainly matches the word *gaudy.*

The rural region we traveled has the "big sky" appearance of Montana, with endless vistas of twenty or thirty miles. How beautiful was the absence of billboards! We practiced our Spanish, with help from our native drivers, brochures of the places we visited, and my old college textbook.

In Salamanca, we received an invitation to visit a hacienda that produces fighting bulls. The owners advised us to come after ten o'clock, when it would be warm enough to ride horseback, so we arranged an early visit to the oldest library in Spain, where many of the manuscripts still have warnings attached that a reader who didn't have special permission from a priest would be excommunicated. There were brilliantly colored maps of the Western Hemisphere dating from a few years after the discovery of the New World.

We drove about forty miles westward to the ranch, or *finca*, owned for many generations by the family of Salustiano Galache Cobalada, whose son Paco guided us on a long ride through carefully separated pastures where bulls were grazing. This family is one of a few who produce the finest bulls, each worth about 1 million pesetas (seven thousand dollars). I was glad that recently I had reread Hemingway's *Death in the Afternoon* and remembered he had said fighting bulls are to domestic ones as wolves are to lapdogs.

We rode around the ranch on horses that were reasonably *"tranquilo"* and relished learning about the step-by-step process that creates those four-year-olds that go into the Spanish bull-rings. There were about seven hundred bulls on the ranch, separated by age. Because they all have a tendency to fight and sometimes kill each other, the older ones are kept in smaller groups, sometimes with steers present. After being separated from his mother as a calf, a bull is never permitted to come in close contact with a cow or a human. We stayed close together, guarded by a picador named Jesus, who kept his horse between us and the bulls we were observing. He was careful to stay away from any lone bull, which might be inclined to charge the horses.

Back at the hacienda, we sat around a table with a thick tablecloth that hung down around us to the floor, a charcoal burner underneath to warm our feet and legs. After a heavy snack of local wines, cheeses, and cured pork ham and tenderloin, we resumed our journey, with stops in Ávila and Segovia.

The next day we left our little bus in Madrid and boarded the bullet train to Seville, a smooth and delightful trip. Until a newer one was put into service in Japan, this was the fastest train in the world, and we enjoyed a visit in the cab with the engineer, who told us about some of the train's characteristics. We were traveling at about 180 miles per hour, and he described the safety precautions and rules. There was a standing offer of a full refund to passengers if the train was five minutes late. In six years, he said, they had never had to make a refund, since rain, fog, or snow didn't affect the train's speed. He admitted, though, that he was nervous the first time he entered a dense fog at top speed.

We found the Alcázar in Seville to be especially beautiful. It has always been under the control of Christians but was built in the fourteenth century by Moorish artisans in their style. The Jews even inserted a few Stars of David into the decorations during those times before the Inquisition.

Throughout Spain there is an intriguing mixture of prehistoric, Roman (time of Christ), Visigoth, Moor, and later Christian history and architecture. There is an earthiness about the country that is distinctive, as Hemingway describes in *For Whom the Bell Tolls*, and a degree of hospitality that surprises visitors. The people seem delighted when anyone speaks their language and ignore the inevitable mistakes.

We spent the night in Carmona, a prehistoric site on a high plateau, the *parador* an old but beautiful building overlooking miles in every direction. It is said that this promontory has been inhabited since prehistoric times, the only place in a wide area that was not covered by ancient seas. In Córdoba, we visited the remarkable mosque-cathedral, one of the prime tourist sites in Spain. There is no way to describe the architectural wonders in this huge building, which covers a square mile and contains eight hundred columns of marble, jasper, and agate. We stopped by to see a famous local vintner, and after I told him that every few years I produce about a hundred liters of wine, he had a case of his superb *vino tinto* delivered to our room at the *parador.* The vice mayor gave us an insider's tour of the *museo de taurinas* and the *plaza de toros.* Manolete, possibly Spain's most famous matador, was from Córdoba, and his life history seems to be known by everyone who lives here. All reports are that the popularity of bullfighting is increasing every year.

The food in the *paradors* and other places was excellent, but we had one of the best meals of our lives at the Caballo Rojo, a restaurant near the mosque. Each dish was new to us, and when I wanted to pay my respects to the chef, the owner insisted that he was the chef to be congratulated, and that he carried all the inherited recipes in his head.

Later, in Granada, we attended an Islamic architectural awards ceremony hosted by the Aga Khan and the royal family. Jeff and Annette enjoyed meeting all the dignitaries, and I sat with people who couldn't speak English and who taught me a lot of Spanish as they questioned me about the Clinton sexual affair, U.S. Cuban policy, the works of Ernest Hemingway, and life in Plains, Georgia.

The next morning we visited the Alhambra complex, guided by the director of archaeology and tourism. This is the most heavily visited place in Europe, and the reasons are obvious. The Alhambra and the adjacent Generalife palace and gardens are wonders to behold.

In Toledo, the *parador* was on a hill across the river from the city, with a breathtaking view similar to the one in El Greco's famous painting. Arriving after most of the tourist sites had closed, we just went shopping through the streets. The *damasquinado* work, with scenes made of inlaid fine gold wire, was especially interesting, and collections of swords, daggers, knives, and scissors were also notable. We asked one of the major shop owners if the factory was open to visitors, and he responded that the next day was Sunday and Monday their biggest holiday, so it would not be possible to see the factory. We left our phone number anyway and soon were informed that the owners would be delighted to open their factory and give us a special tour.

The next morning was the first day of partridge season, and from the balcony we could see hunters and their dogs in the scrub-covered hills around the *parador*. We first visited places where El Greco lived after moving here in 1577 and where many of his remarkable works are displayed in small museums and the great cathedral. The royal family of the time did not support his revolutionary work, so it was done for cathedrals and convents. El Greco has been my favorite artist since I was a child.

Afterward we drove outside the city to the factory where they make weapons and armor. They reproduce the swords of history, literature, and films, including those of Spanish kings, the Moors, Vikings, Christopher Columbus, Charlemagne, Genghis Khan, the Knights Templar, El Cid, Robin Hood, the Three Musketeers, Braveheart, Conan, Hercules, Xena, Highlander, and, of course, Excalibur. We were impressed with the high quality of the steel and the artisanship of the decorations. They offered to make me a Confederate cavalryman's sword like the one used by Robert E. Lee, and a few weeks later it arrived in Plains.

Our group had a heated discussion: "If a visitor could go to only one place in Spain, where should it be?" I would choose Toledo, because of the vitality of the old city, its remarkable appearance from across the river, its vivid history from prehistoric times through the civil war against Franco, shopping, the works of El Greco, and its ambience.

We were in Madrid on October 12, celebrating the National Day of Spain, which to us is Columbus Day. After reviewing a tremendous parade with the royal family and 500,000 other people, we ate lunch at Casa Botín, which Guinness names as the world's oldest restaurant and which is, according to Hemingway, the best. We had *cochinillo asado,* a suckling pig roasted in the eighteenth-century oven. Although the national museum, the Prado, was closed for the holiday, we were invited for a private tour. The many works of Goya, Velázquez, and El Greco are stunningly displayed. I had never seen the incredible black paintings, some quite disturbing, with which the aging Goya covered the walls of his house. We spent our last night at a late supper, watching flamenco dancers.

What made this one of our best vacations was sharing each experience and then comparing our often differing impressions as we drove to our next destination. We tried to find the most accurate words, in both English and Spanish, to express how we felt about past or prospective adventures.

AFRICAN GAME PARKS

S INCE THE CARTER CENTER has so many health and agriculture projects in Africa, we often visit countries where there are wonderful game parks—Kenya, Tanzania, South Africa, Uganda, Zambia, and Swaziland. There are times when Rosalynn and I are traveling alone, as when we drove southwestward from Kampala to visit some of Uganda's game preserves and especially to see the giant mountain gorillas. When we arrived at camp, everyone was examined to assure that we did not have a cold or any other contagious illness that might be transmitted to the wild animals. We were also cautioned not to get too near them or make any disturbing noise or sudden movement—if we were lucky enough to locate the secretive gorillas, who were always moving in extremely rough terrain. Our guides also mentioned that we would be quite near Rwanda, where a civil war was being fought, and that some guerrilla fighters had been sighted in the region.

After a challenging trek from our camp into the heavily forested mountainous region, we found a trampled area of grass

143

and brush where the huge primates had spent the previous night, and we soon came upon a family of at least six gorillas. Our guide placed us on a narrow mountain ledge where we could watch the group. A huge silverback soon climbed a ficus tree about twenty yards from us, completely self-assured and without seeming to notice our presence. He was moving easily from one limb to another, picking and eating bunches of the fruit. A young gorilla, whom the guide said was four years old, climbed about fifteen feet above the ground and reached out for some of the berries. The big male grunted and slapped the youngster, knocking him to the ground, where he lay for a few moments and then disappeared into the brush. We remained still for a half hour, whispering, until two females came into sight, one holding a baby, followed by the youngster. We watched for a while and then quietly withdrew. A few months later, we were startled to learn that Rwandan fighters had raided the camp and killed everyone there.

OF COURSE, all our pleasures are magnified when we can take our children and grandchildren with us. Our first such opportunity came when we climbed Mount Kilimanjaro in 1988 and visited several national game parks. These well-protected refuges gave us a chance to observe many of the most interesting animals in Africa and to learn about them from experienced naturalists.

Since then we have taken a few of our grandchildren on such trips each time another group reaches an appropriate age. Our most recent visit was to Little Governor's Camp in the Masai Mara region of Kenya, where each day we crossed the deep and swift Mara River, which separated our camp from the primary game area. There was a six-passenger wooden boat attached to a rope, by which the boatman pulled hand over hand to cross the stream. Just downriver, there was always a large group of hippopotamuses in the water, and huge crocodiles lay along the bank. It was inevitable that there were a lot of jokes about what would happen if anyone should fall overboard. On our expeditions we sighted a cheetah, giraffes, a large herd of water buffalo, and many other animals but spent a lot of time watching a pride of lions—a male and six females. We saw the lionesses kill a zebra, then back away and lie in the grass, watchful but patient, as the male gorged on the entrails and other tender delicacies.

The next day we saw a lone lioness pursuing a warthog through the thigh-high grasses, and our guide drove our open-sided vehicle to a high mound of earth so we could focus our binoculars on the chase. We were surprised at the erratic and lackadaisical movements of the pursuing lioness, until the guide pointed far ahead, where we spotted a larger lioness lying immobile, her head barely visible above the grass. As an errant lamb driven by a trained sheepdog, the unsuspecting prey was being maneuvered toward its waiting killer. After the dramatic conclusion of the hunt, we drove to within a few yards and watched the dominant lioness eat her fill, growling on occasion when the previous pursuer dared creep in to get a bite. Our grandchildren were especially excited to witness such a vivid example of savagery and survival in the wild.

Whenever anyone sighted a new bird we always stopped and our guides identified it and told us about its habits. In all, we saw 103 different species, forty-four of which were new to Rosalynn and me. One day while returning to camp we sighted the lion with five lionesses and a six-month-old cub crossing the plain, and our drivers got directly ahead of them. Fearing nothing, the male walked in an undeviating straight line and came within eight feet of Jeff and Annette's vehicle before veering away as though he had confronted a small stone wall. As always, we remained still with our arms and legs inside the open-sided vehicle. We were always seeing jackals, hyenas, and various antelope, and that morning there were some bat-eared foxes and an African hare.

At the boat landing, Rosalynn and Annette started across the river on the first trip, while Jeff, their young son Jamie, and I waited on the shore with the second group. When the boat was about halfway across, Jeff picked up a large rock, threw it into the river with a great splash, and yelled, "Jamie! Jamie!" Annette almost fainted with fright, and she still gets furious when anyone mentions the event.

FISHING AND HUNTING
COMPANIONS

LTHOUGH MOST OF our vacation times have been spent together, with or without other members of our family, Rosalynn and I have also enjoyed excursions with a small group of friends. One of our most remarkable companions is Jack Crockford, who was director of the Georgia Game and Fish Department when I was governor. Originally from Michigan, Jack had come to our state as a trained biologist, an expert on mourning doves, bobwhite quail, and other common species, and especially interested in species that had been almost totally eradicated in our region except on a few of the coastal islands.

As a boy, almost constantly in wild areas, I had never seen either a wild turkey or a white-tailed deer. In the years before I was governor, a few turkeys had been caught in cannon-propelled nets by wildlife rangers and distributed to powerful politicians in Atlanta, who either ate them or released them on

147

their small farms, mostly in suburban areas. With my approval, Jack continued to net the turkeys but then liberated them in isolated regions with habitats most amenable to the wild birds' habits. Landowners were not informed that new pairs of turkeys were now dwelling and would be nesting on their property.

The problem with deer was that they were very difficult to capture in the existing large wooden traps and would often injure or kill themselves in a frantic effort to escape. Jack invented the dart gun, which is now used throughout the world to put wild animals into a temporary sleep. While dormant they can be treated for disease, measured and analyzed by expert biologists, transported to areas where additional members of their species are needed, or have transmitters attached so they can be tracked after they return to the wild. The dart gun has been an invaluable tool, as effective with almost all wild animals everywhere as it was in restoring a full population of deer. In fact, the number of both wild turkey and deer in the United States now exceeds what it was when American Indians first began hunting them.

I have spent many days with Jack Crockford. We have hunted woodcock along the shores of the Chattahoochee River, wild turkey on my farm and others, ruffed grouse in Michigan and in the North Georgia mountains, ducks near the coast, and quail in the woods and fields south of my home in Plains. His quiet comments about flora and fauna have been constant lessons, and have helped to shape my concerns about the protection of wildlife.

Jack is a superb artisan in wood and metal, and his handcrafted knives are sold in the finest sporting shops. For my fiftieth birthday, he made a muzzle-loaded rifle for me, with powder horn and other appurtenances, and taught me to load and fire it. It is one of my prized possessions, which I have proudly displayed at the governor's office, in the White House, and now at home.

DURING OUR FIRST FEW YEARS back in Plains, I also enjoyed quail hunting with Sam Walton, the founder of Wal-Mart. He was fascinated with the sport and remarked, not completely in jest, that he spent the year as a manager: nine months running his skyrocketing business and three months running his bird dogs. We hunted near my home in South Georgia, but most seasons we flew to Texas, where he and his brother leased hunting rights on a large tract of prairie land, covered mostly with mesquite and cactus. Sam had a small twin-engine airplane, which was less for human passengers than for his four dogs. They ran freely throughout the cabin, which had the overpowering odor of a kennel.

In the still dark morning, Sam was awake and on the telephone with his headquarters in Arkansas, discussing the prices and quantities of individual sale items. I was also awake, able to hear every word through the paper-thin walls of the dilapidated house trailer that formed his camp: "The men's corduroy jackets are not moving. Cut the price to $13.95." After breakfast, we would be lined up at the edge of his property, waiting for enough daylight so we wouldn't step on one of the rattlesnakes or into a gopher hole. Sam always refused to ride on a horse or in a Jeep, preferring to walk all day behind his dogs, never slowing except when there was a point. I was jogging long distances in those days and was more than ten years his junior, but it was very difficult for me to match his pace after the first few hours.

I always enjoyed being with Sam Walton and having a chance for eight or more hours each day to discuss matters of common interest. Above anyone else I've ever known, he was able to combine his remarkable dedication to retail marketing with the challenge and pleasure of training his own pointers and setters and following them in the fields and prairies.

IN RECENT YEARS, Rosalynn and I have turned increasingly from hunting to fly-fishing, and we have a number of friends who share our love for the sport. We spend a few days each year with Ted Turner, driving from one of his Montana ranches to another, depending on the changing weather and condition of the streams. Ted is also a fascinating companion, always exploring new and innovative ideas, quoting his own poetry, and expounding on politics, philosophy, international affairs, environmental issues, baseball, and the continuing threat of uncontrolled nuclear weapons. Now the largest private landowner in America, he takes extraordinary steps to beautify each tract of land that he acquires, removes most of the existing fences, replaces cattle with bison, and turns his properties into perpetual nature preserves. Since fly-fishing is a solitary pursuit and we rarely see each other on the stream, we have our conversations while he's driving his Land Rover or at night, when we all share accounts of our day's adventures.

• • •

I'VE ALSO FORMED an informal fishing alliance with Wayne Harpster from Spruce Creek, the marine contractor Bob Wilson from North Carolina, Carlton Hicks, an optometrist from the Georgia coast, and the software entrepreneur John Moores, who owns the San Diego Padres. In addition to streams in the eastern states, Colorado, and Alaska, we have fished together for peacock bass in the Orinoco River in southern Venezuela, and in Argentina's Tierra del Fuego for sea-run brown trout, which leave the freshwater streams and spend a portion of their lives at sea. They become several times larger than their less adventurous siblings who remain in the fresh water.

Rosalynn and some of the wives join this group when possible, and in July 2004 we particularly enjoyed a visit to the Kamchatka peninsula in Russia, where we spent six days floating down the Zhupanova River, stopping frequently to wade and cast for large and powerful rainbow trout. This was an especially wild region, 125 miles from the nearest house, and we were surprised to learn that we were nearer New York than Moscow.

A special relationship develops among friends who share experiences like these, with opportunities to visit new and exotic places, to know people who live completely different kinds of lives, to learn from them and from each other, to enjoy friendly competition each day, to observe the reactions of companions to stress, relaxation, achievement, and failure, and to reveal in unguarded moments the personal characteristics that are customarily concealed from others. There is, of necessity, a careful and subtle screening process so that the final unanimous choice—at least for the next trip—is of companions who are completely compatible.

•   •   •

ROSALYNN AND I ALSO have stayed close to the people who
campaigned with us and then served in my administrations,
both as governor and as president. Many of them join us in carrying out the projects of The Carter Center, and we visit them
as we travel to different cities.

All of these lasting relationships are sources of joy, but two
have evolved into an annual ceremony. Jody Powell was my
driver when I campaigned for governor, and he served as press
secretary in Atlanta and in Washington. Frank Moore became
executive director of a seven-county planning commission that I
formed in the 1960s and later served as executive secretary in
the governor's office and as liaison officer with the Congress
when I was president. After we all left the White House, the
Powells and Moores acquired a site on the Eastern Shore of the
Chesapeake, built two houses, and developed the lowlands and
woodlands into a superb habitat for wildlife.

In the late fall or winter, Jody, Frank, and their wives invite
us up for a few days. We men usually go out early to get a few
ducks, and for the rest of the day all of us enjoy hiking, fishing,
boating, and long and relaxed conversations in front of an open
fire. We have made a new circle of friends among the residents
in the community, including game and fish specialists and local
fishermen, farmers, and merchants. At least once during each
visit, there is an oyster roast and picnic to which our hosts invite
several dozen guests.

Since the Powells and Moores have not yet fulfilled their ultimate plans to live there year-round, they give us a comprehen-

sive insight into current Washington political and social life—at least from a Democratic point of view. To Rosalynn and me, after nearly a quarter century away from the nation's capital, this is an intriguing glimpse into the almost totally different world of partisan politics.

PRIVATE HOBBIES

ESPITE MY ENJOYMENT in the company of other
people, there are some things I prefer to do alone, including woodworking, painting, and writing. When I
was a boy we had a blacksmith shop on our farm, where my father made and repaired tools, wagon wheels, and other equipment, sharpened plows and hoes, and shoed the mules and
horses. This was also where he kept his carpenter's tools, moving larger projects outside the small building onto sawhorses
when he needed more elbow room. There was also a cobbler's
bench tucked away in a corner and iron lasts on which he repaired our family's shoes. In front of the shop, always available
for anyone on the farm, was a large grinding wheel, propelled by
pedals similar to a bicycle's and used to sharpen knives, scissors,
hoes, and other items.

This was a very busy and intriguing place when I was a child,
and as often as possible I followed Daddy when I knew he was
heading to the shop. One of my earliest jobs was to work the
bellows that sent a stream of air up through the burning char-

coal to bring iron almost to the melting point, while he held the metal in tongs until it was malleable enough for shaping. Then, if I was able, I would hold the item on the anvil with the tongs while he beat on it with a sledgehammer before dousing it in water or oil to obtain the correct hardness and toughness.

Eventually, I learned most of the blacksmithing chores and was proud of my grown-up responsibilities, but it was the woodworking tools that really appealed to me. Most of the work in the shop was making handles for hoes, shovels, and rakes, and repairing wagon tongues, singletrees, and parts of the plows. During the wintertime we repaired the various buildings on the farm, replacing wooden steps, doors and window frames, or leaking roofs.

All of us farm boys became members of the Future Farmers of America when we reached the eighth grade, and one of our responsibilities was to improve the skills we had learned at home. For the finer aspects of woodworking, such as making furniture, the school shop was much more spacious and better equipped than the one we had at the farm, and I learned there how to make relatively simple chairs, tables, and cabinets. We had local, congressional district, and statewide contests in some of these skills.

As a naval officer stationed in Hawaii, I had access to some of the navy's fully equipped "hobby shops," usually manned by warrant officers who were expert cabinetmakers. From them I learned the finer points of working with different kinds of woods, making well-structured joints, using proper glues, and finishing the surfaces. I enjoyed designing pieces of furniture, and Rosalynn and I were able to rent cheaper apartments by furnishing them with chairs, beds, and tables that I had made myself. I left most of these pieces behind when we came back to the mainland, but Rosalynn and I still own a few pieces from those early days.

Back in Plains, I had limited access to proper tools and facilities and made cruder but serviceable furniture, but I still had a desire to improve my abilities. When we prepared to leave the White House in January 1981, my White House staff and the members of my cabinet took up a collection to buy me a going-away gift. When I learned that they were planning to purchase a Jeep, I sent word that this was not something I wanted, with a hint that furniture making was what I would like to resume. My friends then gave the same funds to Sears, Roebuck and Co., with directions to supply me with whatever tools and equipment I needed for a completely furnished woodworking shop in what had been our garage.

This has turned out to be one of the best gifts of my life, and I have devoted a good portion of my spare time to developing my skills and designing and building furniture. On the all-too-rare days we have at home in Plains, I devote the early morning hours to reading incoming e-mail, scanning the major newspapers on the Internet, and then writing on whatever book or poem is of most interest at the time. When I tire of the computer screen, I can walk twenty steps to my woodshop and immerse myself in my current project. I traveled very seldom during my first year back from Washington, and had time enough to write my presidential memoir and to build all the furniture needed for our cabin in North Georgia. Since then, I have designed and built more than one hundred items, ranging from small stools to large four-poster beds.

Each year for the piece I contribute to The Carter Center to be auctioned, I take a series of about two dozen photographs, from selecting the rough boards on to finishing the surface and burning my signature in some out-of-the-way place. One year I carved a chess set and nestled the pieces in a small case that Rosalynn lined with velvet. There has always been spirited bidding for these artifacts from a president's workshop, and prices have ranged from fifty thousand dollars to more than five times as much.

One of my most productive family projects has been the crafting of cradles for three of our children, to encourage them to produce more grandchildren for us. Subsequently, the cradles have been loaned to their friends, who show off both their new babies and the cradles. When our church needs collection plates, small tables and chairs for the nursery, portable bookshelves, or television cabinets, I'm always available. Also, Rosalynn has been in charge of decorating a new inn and café in Plains, and I've honored her requests for tall cabinets and long serving tables.

As with our other hobbies, woodworking has brought another circle of new friends. I have attended workshops or consulted personally with some of the world's finest artisans, both in America and in Europe and the Orient, primarily to admire their work but also to learn more advanced techniques. Everyone who shares my interest would recognize the names of Sam Maloof, Tage Frid, and Ed Moulthrop, three gurus who have shared their talents with so many students and admirers.

When we travel in Third World countries, I try to visit some of the more renowned woodworkers. One of the most interesting has a large shop in Accra, Ghana, which we usually take our traveling companions to visit on trips to our Center's projects in the country. With a team of ten assistants, this master craftsman produces burial caskets of various shapes to match the special interests of the deceased. There are carrots, hot peppers, or ears of corn for farmers; boats, fish, squid, or different kinds of sea life for fishermen; and automobiles, buses, or airplanes if the customers have these special interests. His most interesting addition on our last visit was a jogging shoe, with carefully crafted tongue and strings, in which one of Ghana's Olympic runners plans to be interred.

I have been delighted that two of my sons and three grandsons take an interest in woodworking, and I've taught them how to use most of my tools and given them their own. Chip does most of the renovation and repair work in his home, and Jeff and his boys have recently added a large wooden deck behind his house. All the grandchildren join me in making simple toys, and Joshua has used my lathe to turn Christmas presents for his mother and girlfriend. In return, Rosalynn and I depend on them to make the advanced adjustments and program entries on our television sets, DVD players, radios, and computers.

ANOTHER HOBBY that I have enjoyed is painting. In my first naval assignment on an old battleship, one of my many duties was as the education officer, and I was responsible for helping sailors qualify for high school diplomas, complete college courses, or just study subjects of interest to them. One of the sailors ordered a course in art history and beginner's oil paints, but he resigned from the navy before his materials arrived, so I inherited them. This was my introduction to art as I experimented with the paints from time to time.

Lately I have become more serious about this commitment and have acquired more artists' materials and a collection of how-to books on painting landscapes, still lifes, and portraits. I'm still in the learning stage but have really enjoyed the new challenge. I've set up an easel in a corner of my woodshop and now have a choice between woodworking and painting when I take a respite from writing. I've done a satisfactory portrait of Rosalynn, painted the cover of my novel, *The Hornet's Nest,* and produced a triple portrait of Sadat, Begin, and me at the 1979 signing ceremony of the peace treaty between Egypt and Israel. The last painting was given to The Carter Center in lieu of a piece of furniture for its annual auction.

I plan to continue my efforts as an author, woodworker, and artist, hoping to improve the quality of my work in all these pursuits. Two of these are just hobbies, but my books have provided the major portion of our family's income since I left the White House.

MY FIRST OF NINETEEN published books was *Why Not the Best?* which I wrote during 1975, mostly while I was traveling throughout the country during the earliest phase of my campaign for president. I wrote on airplanes and in hotel rooms at night, by hand on a yellow legal pad, then typed the text during my weekend visits back to Plains.

This was a brief book about my early life, my governorship, and my vision for America. I couldn't find a publisher when it was finished but finally persuaded Broadman Press, which printed Baptist Sunday school literature, to bring it out. There was no advance payment, but they agreed to give me a certain percentage of the proceeds from the books they were able to sell. We tried to peddle as many as possible for five dollars and handed out the others to my early supporters. Later, after I won the primary contests in Iowa, New Hampshire, and Florida, Broadman could not manage all the orders, and Bantam took the title over and sold more than a million copies.

I spent the first year after leaving the White House perusing six thousand pages of detailed diary notes and wrote my presidential memoir, *Keeping Faith.* By this time I had a rudimentary word processor, and I really enjoyed both the research and the writing. A year later Rosalynn wrote *First Lady from Plains,* which was number one on the *New York Times* bestseller list. (My memoir was number three, after *Megatrends* and Jane Fonda's workout book.) The income from our two books helped to pay off a surprising debt that had been accumulated by our blind trust while we were in Washington and opened the door to a new profession for us both.

A few years later we hosted a major international meeting at The Carter Center, where more than a hundred experts on health care assembled to assess how little of our knowledge about proper personal habits is actually put into practice in our daily lives. The title of our conference was Closing the Gap, and there was a consensus that the findings would be much more widely distributed if Rosalynn and I would write a book pulling them all together.

This seemed like a good idea, and we decided to personalize the text as much as possible, describing some of the events in our lives and interweaving the lessons that our conference had produced. We signed a publishing contract and began our work. Rosalynn and I have different workrooms, each furnished with a computer and some bookshelves and filing cabinets. Mine was in our old garage and hers in one of the rooms vacated when our boys moved away.

The joint project soon turned out to be a disaster, however, and came as near as any other experience to destroying the harmony of our marriage. With the help of our editor, we had divided the chapter topics, with the idea of my writing the first version of half and Rosalynn taking the others. As we began to describe even the most simple and basic events of our years together, we found that we could finally agree on perhaps 97 percent of the facts, but we had irreconcilable differences about the others, either what actually happened or our reaction to them. Topics of the resulting arguments even included our first date, as well as our early years in the navy, whether events had seemed happy or sad, and much else that we had experienced together.

Another problem was that I write very rapidly, and Rosalynn labors over every sentence until she is satisfied. When I gave her my texts, she almost inevitably considered them rough drafts eagerly awaiting her drastic editing. She considered her proposed texts, however, to have the same status as the Ten Commandments brought down by Moses from Mount Sinai, and any change was almost a personal insult. We soon found that we could communicate about our book only by writing ugly notes back and forth on our computers.

After a few weeks we decided to abandon the book and return the advance, but our editor, Peter Osnos, asked us to give it one more try. He took all the paragraphs on which we disagreed and divided them between us, and each of us agreed not to dispute what the other had written. In the final version, there is an initial, either "R" or "J," alongside many sections to indicate who wrote the final version of each. Understandably, we also agreed never to write another book together. We've had no further problems, and we edit each other's speeches, editorials, and books. The solution is that the author always makes the final decision.

When I wrote a children's book, *The Little Baby Snoogle-Fleejer,* our daughter, Amy, did the illustrations, working for three hundred hours to produce thirteen large pastels. My granddaughter Sarah Elizabeth illustrated my book of poetry, *Always a Reckoning,* with pen-and-ink drawings of the forty-two subjects. Although she had helped pay her way through school by doing quick portraits of people at vacation sites, I had to assist her when the poems were about objects she had never seen: a mule, a wooden fence, a submarine, or a nurse's cap. I called on Amy again to produce the illustrations for *Christmas in Plains.* In all these joint endeavors I learned a lot from the young women, and they went with me on the book tours, for signings in bookstores and television appearances on *Larry King Live* or *Good Morning America.* Sarah attracted more attention than I, in fact, because at the time she had her hair dyed purple.

In addition to the books, I enjoy writing magazine and newspaper articles that describe some of our experiences and express my views about current events. As advanced age brings an end to mountain climbing, downhill skiing, jogging, and even tennis, my hope is that swimming, writing, painting, woodworking, fishing, and bird watching will help keep us physically fit and intellectually challenged.

CONCLUSION

I T IS QUITE NATURAL that our family has had some of these experiences because I was president and am in charge of The Carter Center's projects in many foreign countries. The fact is, however, that our most memorable adventures have been those that were available when our family was living in a government housing project and had a very low income. We had to learn in those days how to reach out to our own children and our friends in order to stretch our hearts and minds with new challenges and adventures, always seeking ways to share pleasures with others.

As did my parents in the same farming community, we were forced to accommodate seasonal opportunities in shaping a proper relationship between times of work and times of recreation. Quite belatedly, Rosalynn and I strengthened our marriage ties by forming a multitude of personal partnerships in the fields and woodlands, in our business office, on the political campaign trail, and in our worldwide activities.

I can see the long and sometimes faltering evolution toward

a partnership of complete equality, in which we share all possible activities and never make a family decision without a thorough discussion and a mutual decision reached in harmony. After fifty-eight years together, we've both learned that our own happiness is predicated on a flexible relationship, trying always to communicate with each other, even during unpleasant times.

Rosalynn and I still relish the days when just the two of us are at home together. We do our own things most of the time, but share responsibilities in the house, the yard, and around the outdoor grill. We work out in a nearby gym, swim, ride bikes, or take a long walk every day, and we're highly competitive while fishing in one of our ponds or playing tennis. I have a stronger serve, her ground strokes are more accurate, and neither of us would dream of exerting less than our full effort. We have developed a formula for equalizing the odds, so that every set is likely to come out about even.

During one of our joint television interviews as we passed an anniversary, we were asked to explain how our marriage had been so enduring. Before I could respond, Rosalynn said, "We've learned to give each other enough space to be different." I was somewhat surprised at first but quickly realized that this was one of the best lessons we had learned. Through trials and errors, we learned what we wanted to do together and when either one of us wanted to do our own thing.

Over time Rosalynn and I have attempted deliberately to find more and more things to do together, and we have extended this desire to other members of our family. Building this relationship has not been easy, and it's still a challenge—but it's always worthwhile. With each succeeding year, it has become increasingly important to consider what would bring more plea-sure to other members of our family, and this inclination is shared by our children for their children. The natural result has been an orientation toward the younger ones, with more and more of our own pleasure coming vicariously as we relish the enjoyment and happiness of others.

We visited the Galápagos Islands in August 2004, and our five-year-old grandson, Hugo, was the center of attention. Our enjoyment was almost exclusively determined by his reactions to the mammoth tortoises grazing like cattle, the dozens of cavort-ing sea lions, the brilliant red or blue feet of boobies, the mating dances of wave albatross, or the multicolored marine iguanas.

Learning to share in this way has been one of the most grati-fying experiences of my life.

ACKNOWLEDGMENTS

THIS BOOK HAS TRULY BEEN a joint family affair, with inputs from Rosalynn, our children and in-laws, and especially our grandchildren, as we recalled our favorite memories of the fun times we've had together. My boyhood friends have also joined in some of the discussions, and I am grateful to them for first introducing me to the joy of sharing.

My personal recollections were often surprising and sometimes painful, as I was forced to reexamine my more egocentric years, driven by ambition to exclude even my closest loved ones as I made unilateral decisions that affected their lives. My wife was tolerant and patient during our early times together as I learned to overcome this inclination so we could enjoy life together.

Faye Perdue and Nancy Konigsmark helped ensure that trip reports and diary notes were available to cover my activities during the past twenty-five years. In addition, Faye was a helpful conduit to my literary agent, Lynn Nesbit, and to my publishers at Simon & Schuster. My editor, Alice Mayhew, once again has played a vital role as a tough critic, a wise adviser, and a good friend.

INDEX

ABOUT THE AUTHOR

JIMMY CARTER, who served as thirty-ninth President of the United States, was born in Plains, Georgia, in 1924. After leaving the White House, he and his wife, Rosalynn, founded the Atlanta-based Carter Center, a nonprofit organization that works to prevent and resolve conflicts, enhance freedom and democracy, and improve health around the world. The author of numerous books, including the bestselling memoir *An Hour Before Daylight,* Jimmy Carter was awarded the 2002 Nobel Peace Prize.